Crescent Books
New York

The following trademarks appearing in this cookbook are owned by and identify
products of PET INCORPORATED, ST. LOUIS, MO 63102. (An IC Industries Company):
PET, WHITMAN'S, WHITMAN'S SAMPLER, SAMPLER, the WHITMAN'S SAMPLER design,
PET-RITZ, HEARTLAND, LA CREME, DOWNYFLAKE.

Created and manufactured by arrangement with
Ottenheimer Publishers, Inc. under license from Whitman's Chocolates Division, Pet Incorporated
(An IC Industries Company).

This 1987 edition is published by Ottenheimer
Publishers, Inc. for Crescent Books,
distributed by Crown Publishers, Inc., 225 Park
Avenue South, New York, New York, 10003.

Printed in U.S.A.

h g f e d c b a
ISBN 0-517-64157-7

Library of Congress Cataloging in Publication Data

Whitman's chocolate cookbook.

Includes index.
1. Cookery (Chocolate) I. Hoffman, Marian.
TX767.C5W47 1987 641.8'6 87-9016
ISBN 0-517-64157-7

Contents

The History of Whitman's

In 1842, Stephen F. Whitman set up a small confectionery store near Philadelphia's waterfront. Sailors brought him the imported fruits, nuts, cocoa, and flavorings he needed to create a product that could compete with the expensive European candies that were in great demand at the time.

Whitman's quickly became first a regional, then a national success. By 1866, Whitman's thriving business needed larger quarters, and took over an entire building at 12th and Market Streets in Philadelphia. In 1876, Whitman's received an award at the Philadelphia Centennial Celebration. It was also given international recognition at the Paris Exposition in 1878.

A key factor to Whitman's success was its innovative marketing techniques. A pioneer in newspaper and magazine advertising, Stephen Whitman placed his first newspaper ad before the Civil War and was advertising regularly in magazines before the turn of the century. Whitman's was among the first to introduce packaged confections in printed boxes. And it was the first candy company to use cellophane wrapping in the packaging of its product.

Whitman's most successful innovation was the introduction of WHITMAN'S SAMPLER in 1912. Walter P. Sharp, the third president of Whitman's, decided that the linen background and designs of an old embroidered sampler he had hanging in his home would make a beautiful candy box. His WHITMAN'S SAMPLER soon became the best-selling box of prestige candy in the country. It was the first box of candy to come with its own index—a diagram in the box lid showing what was in each candy. Three years after the introduction of the SAMPLER came the famous WHITMAN'S MESSENGER BOY.

Today, Whitman's plant and offices are located on thirty-seven acres in Philadelphia. In 1963, Whitman's became an operating division of Pet,

Incorporated, which was acquired by IC Industries in 1978. The Whitman's Division of Pet, Incorporated markets chocolate chips, baking chocolate, hard candy sticks, Danish butter cookies, and special holiday items for Easter, Christmas, and Valentine's Day, as well as its traditional, much-loved chocolates.

The History of Chocolate

Although Columbus was the first to bring cacao beans from America to Europe, it was the Spanish explorer Cortez who first realized the commercial possibilities of the cacao beans.

During his conquest of Mexico, Cortez discovered that Emperor Montezuma II served his guests golden goblets filled with a bitter drink called "chocolati," made from cacao beans. Cortez took the chocolate drink back to Spain, where it was sweetened with sugar, cinnamon, and vanilla and became a favorite of the Spanish aristocracy, who believed it to be an aphrodisiac. Spain then planted cacao trees in her colonies and developed a lucrative business that was kept secret for almost a century. Eventually, the formula was leaked to Italy, and from there chocolate fever spread to France, Holland, and the British Isles. The chocolate drink became so popular in England that special Chocolate Houses were established.

An important milestone for the chocolate industry occurred in 1876 when Daniel Peter of Switzerland added milk to chocolate and invented a way to make solid chocolate. The introduction of machines that ground and processed the cacao beans and ones that automatically shaped the centers and poured just the right amount of liquid chocolate over them helped catapult chocolate to its present popularity.

From Cacao Beans to Chocolate

Cacao beans are the fruit of the cacao tree, which grows mainly in Latin America and West Africa. To make chocolate, the cacao beans are first cleaned, then roasted at a carefully controlled temperature. Their outer shells are taken off, leaving the cacao nibs, which are more than 50 percent cocoa butter.

When the nibs are ground, enough heat is generated to liquify the cocoa butter, creating chocolate liquor. Pure chocolate liquor cooled and molded into blocks, is **unsweetened baking chocolate.**

Using high pressure, most of the cocoa butter is extracted from the chocolate liquor, leaving **cocoa powder.** Cocoa will stay fresh almost indefinitely without refrigeration if it's stored in a tightly closed jar.

Semisweet chocolate is made from at least 35 percent chocolate liquor, cocoa butter, and sugar. **Sweet dark chocolate** has the same ingredients as semisweet chocolate, but has at least 15 percent chocolate liquor and a higher sugar content.

Milk is combined with at least 10 percent chocolate liquor, cocoa butter, and sugar to make **milk chocolate.**

Foods that are flavored with cocoa or chocolate liquor but do not have enough of these ingredients to be considered chocolate are labeled **"chocolate flavored." White chocolate** is not really chocolate at all—the cocoa butter has been removed and replaced by a different vegetable fat, and there is no chocolate liquor in it.

Chocolate Conversion Chart

Unsweetened Baking Chocolate				
3 level tablespoons cocoa	+	**1 tablespoon shortening (liquid or solid)**	=	**1 ounce or 1 square unsweetened baking chocolate**

SemiSweet Baking Chocolate				
6 level tablespoons cocoa	+	**7 tablespoons sugar** **1/4 cup shortening**	=	**6-ounce package (1 cup) semisweet chocolate chips** **or** **6 blocks (1 ounce each) semisweet baking chocolate**

Sweet Baking Chocolate				
3 level tablespoons cocoa	+	**4 1/2 tablespoons sugar** **2 2/3 tablespoons shortening**	=	**1 bar (4 ounces) sweet baking chocolate**

For Successful Recipes

Each recipe in this cookbook has been thoroughly tested in the Pet Kitchens in St. Louis, Missouri using PET products. For successful results in your kitchen . . .

When the recipe calls for:	**Use:**
evaporated milk	PET Evaporated Milk
frozen pie crust shells	PET-RITZ Frozen Pie Crust Shells
frozen deep-dish pie crust shells	PET-RITZ Deep-Dish Frozen Pie Crust Shells
frozen graham cracker pie crust	PET-RITZ Graham Cracker Pie Crust
waffles	DOWNYFLAKE Waffles
natural cereal—plain, raisin or coconut variety	HEARTLAND Natural Cereal—plain, raisin or coconut variety
milk chocolate bars	WHITMAN'S All Natural Milk Chocolate Bars
whipped topping	LA CREME Whipped Topping with real cream

Cakes

Chocolate Roulage

MAKES 10 TO 12 SERVINGS

1 4-ounce bar sweet cooking chocolate
4 ounces (4 squares) semisweet chocolate
⅓ cup cold water
8 eggs, separated
1 cup sugar
Cocoa
1½ cups whipping cream
3 tablespoons confectioners' sugar, sifted
1 teaspoon vanilla

Preheat oven to 350° F. Oil bottom of a 15½ × 10½ × 1-inch jelly roll pan. Cut piece of waxed paper to fit width of pan and extend about 1 inch over ends.

Place chocolates and water in top of double boiler over hot water. Stir with wooden spoon until chocolate is melted, then cool. Place egg yolks in large mixer bowl and beat slightly with mixer. Add sugar gradually, beating constantly until all sugar is dissolved and mixture is thick and of a batter consistency. Stir in chocolate with rubber spatula until well combined and free of streaks. Beat egg whites until stiff peaks form. Fold about ⅓ of the egg whites into chocolate mixture thoroughly to lighten, then fold in remaining egg whites carefully but completely with rubber spatula.

Spread batter evenly in prepared pan. Bake for 18 minutes. Remove from oven and cover top with damp towels. Let stand for 30 minutes or until cooled. Remove towels carefully, then loosen by lifting extending ends of waxed paper. Place cocoa in fine sieve and dust top generously. Place piece of waxed paper over top, then place cookie sheet on top and invert. Peel waxed paper carefully from cake.

Place cream in large mixer bowl and beat with electric mixer until soft peaks form. Sprinkle in confectioners' sugar and beat until stiff. Stir in vanilla. Spread whipped cream evenly over cake.

Roll cake from the long side, as for a jelly roll, directly onto a serving tray. Roll with care as this cake is extremely delicate. Dust top generously with cocoa. You may refrigerate roll for several hours before serving. Cut into slices to serve.

German Chocolate Cake

MAKES 8 TO 10 SERVINGS

1 cup milk
1 tablespoon lemon juice
1 bar (4 ounces) sweet baking chocolate
1½ cups all-purpose flour, sifted
1 teaspoon baking soda
½ teaspoon salt
¾ cup butter or margarine, softened
1 cup sugar
2 eggs
1 teaspoon vanilla

Preheat oven to 350°F. Line two 8-inch round baking pans with waxed paper.

Blend milk and lemon juice. Set aside. Melt chocolate in double boiler. Cool slightly. Sift flour, baking soda, and salt together. In large mixing bowl, cream butter. Add sugar, then eggs and vanilla. Blend in half of dry ingredients. Stir in milk mixture and melted chocolate. Mix in remaining dry ingredients.

Pour into prepared baking pans. Bake 30 to 40 minutes, or until toothpick inserted in center comes out clean. Cool completely before frosting with Caramel Coconut Frosting.

Caramel Coconut Frosting

⅔ cup milk
1 egg
⅔ cup brown sugar, firmly packed
½ cup butter or margarine, softened
1 teaspoon vanilla
1 cup coconut, shredded

In 1-quart saucepan, heat and stir milk, egg, brown sugar, and butter until bubbly and thick. Chill until cold and thick. Beat in vanilla and coconut. Frost cooled cake.

Chocolate Chip Angel Cake

MAKES 12 SERVINGS

1 angel food cake mix
½ cup chocolate chips, finely chopped
1 quart hand-dipped vanilla ice cream
1 cup Hot Fudge Sauce (see Index)

Prepare cake mix as directed. Fold in chocolate chips. Bake as directed. Cool. Slice into serving pieces. Spoon ice cream into serving dish; place in center of large serving tray. Arrange cake slices around ice cream.

Heat Hot Fudge Sauce. Serve with cake and ice cream.

German Chocolate Cake

Banana Chocolate Chip Cupcakes

MAKES 2 DOZEN CUPCAKES

1¾ cups all-purpose flour
1¼ cups sugar
3 teaspoons baking powder
½ teaspoon salt
½ cup shortening, softened
¾ cup (about 2 medium) bananas, mashed
⅓ cup milk
2 teaspoons vanilla
2 eggs
½ package (6 ounces) semisweet chocolate chips

Preheat oven to 375° F. In large bowl, stir flour, sugar, baking powder, and salt together. Add shortening, bananas, milk, vanilla, and eggs all at once. Beat until blended with an electric mixer, then beat 3 minutes on medium speed. Stir in chocolate chips.

Pour batter into muffin cups, filling about ¾ full. Bake 20 minutes, or until cupcakes test done when a toothpick inserted in center comes out clean. Remove from pan. Let cool on rack.

Black Bottom Cupcakes

MAKES 18 CUPCAKES

1½ cups all-purpose flour, sifted
1 cup sugar
¼ cup cocoa
1 teaspoon baking soda
½ teaspoon salt
1 cup water
⅓ cup salad oil
1 tablespoon distilled white vinegar
1 teaspoon vanilla

Cream Cheese Filling
1 package (8 ounces) cream cheese
1 egg
½ cup sugar
⅛ teaspoon salt
1 cup (6-ounce package) semisweet chocolate pieces

Preheat oven to 350° F. Sift flour, sugar, cocoa, soda, and salt together. Add water, oil, vinegar, and vanilla. Beat well. Fill paper-lined muffin cups one half full. Beat cream cheese and egg together. Mix in sugar and salt, then stir in chocolate pieces. Spoon cream-cheese mixture on top of batter in muffin cups.

Bake about 30 to 35 minutes, until toothpick inserted in cocoa portion comes out clean. Remove from muffin pans. Let cool on wire rack. Store in refrigerator.

Chocolate Chip Cupcakes

MAKES 32 CUPCAKES

1 cup butter, softened
12 tablespoons granulated sugar
12 tablespoons brown sugar
1 teaspoon vanilla
2 to 3 eggs
2 cups plus 4 tablespoons flour, sifted
1 teaspoon baking soda
1 teaspoon salt

Topping
1 cup brown sugar
2 eggs
¼ teaspoon salt
2 cups chocolate chips
1 cup walnuts, chopped
1 teaspoon vanilla

Preheat oven to 375° F. Line muffin cups with paper.

Combine and cream butter, granulated sugar, 12 tablespoons brown sugar, and 1 teaspoon of vanilla. Beat in eggs. Add flour, baking soda, and salt. Put 1 tablespoon of this mixture in prepared muffin cup.

To make topping, combine brown sugar, eggs, and salt; beat until thick. Add chocolate chips, walnuts, and vanilla. Spoon 1 tablespoon topping mixture over each cupcake. Bake cupcakes 10 minutes, then cover with topping again and bake 2 minutes more.

Triple Chocolate Stacks

MAKES 2 DOZEN CUPCAKES

1¾ cups sugar
⅔ cup margarine, softened
3 eggs
1 teaspoon vanilla
2½ cups all-purpose flour
1½ teaspoons baking soda
¼ teaspoon salt
1 cup sour milk
2 packets liquid chocolate
½ cup boiling water
Chocolate Icing (see Index)
½ cup chocolate sprinkles

Preheat oven to 350° F. Line muffin cups with paper.

Cream sugar and margarine until light and fluffy. Add eggs individually, beating well after each addition. Mix in vanilla. Sift dry ingredients together; add to creamed mixture alternately with sour milk. Dissolve chocolate in boiling water; add to batter. Mix well.

Fill muffin cups ⅔ full of batter. Bake for 25 minutes, or until done. Cool. Prepare icing; frost top of cooled cupcakes. Sprinkle chocolate sprinkles on top.

Spaceship Cake

MAKES 10 SERVINGS

1 1-layer chocolate cake mix
2 cups almonds, slivered
5 tablespoons hot water
½ cup light corn syrup
¼ cup margarine, melted
2 cups chocolate chips
2½ cups Hot Fudge Sauce (can be used in place of last 4 ingredients above) (see Index)

Preheat oven to 350° F.

Prepare cake mix as directed. Pour batter into long, shallow loaf pan. Bake cake for 20 minutes, or until done. Cool slightly before removing from pan. Place cake on rack, top-side-down. With sharp knife, cut off sharp corners of cake. Stick almonds into cake in a staggered row design. Cover to prevent drying.

Combine hot water, corn syrup, and margarine in top of a double boiler. Bring mixture to a boil. Continue to boil until margarine melts. Remove from heat; stir in chocolate chips. Beat until sauce is combined. (Or, heat Hot Fudge Sauce over a double boiler until it drips from a spoon.) Cool sauce to warm; spoon *slowly* over cake with almonds. (This process must be done slowly to allow the sauce time to adhere to the nuts and cake.) Allow sauce to set before serving.

Chocolate Cake

MAKES ABOUT 10 SERVINGS

2 eggs
1¼ cups sugar
4 tablespoons cocoa
⅔ cup flour
7 tablespoons butter or margarine, melted
¼ teaspoon salt

Mocha Cream Filling
3½ tablespoons butter
⅓ cup confectioners' sugar
2 tablespoons strong coffee

Topping
¾ cup whipping cream
Slivered cooking chocolate
Tiny candies, optional

Preheat oven to 350° F. Grease springform cake pan and sprinkle with bread crumbs.

Mix eggs and sugar together, but do not beat. Add cocoa, flour, butter, and salt. Stir until batter is no longer lumpy. Pour into prepared pan. Bake for about 25 minutes. The cake should not be entirely dry.

To make cream filling, stir butter, confectioners' sugar, and coffee into a smooth cream. It should have a strong coffee flavor.

Spread cream filling over the cold cake, which has not been removed from bottom of cake pan. Spread whipped cream on top and sprinkle with slivered cooking chocolate. Garnish with tiny candies. Serve cake cold.

Chocolate Cake

Truly Different Cupcakes

MAKES 2 DOZEN CUPCAKES

1 cup butter or margarine
4 ounces (4 squares) unsweetened baking chocolate
1 cup nuts, chopped
1¾ cups sugar
1 cup all-purpose flour
1 teaspoon vanilla
4 eggs

Preheat oven to 325° F. Line 2-inch muffin cups with paper.

In double boiler, melt butter and chocolate together over medium heat. Stir in nuts. In bowl, combine sugar, flour, vanilla, and eggs. Blend in chocolate mixture by hand, being careful not to overmix.

Pour batter into muffin cups, filling ½ to ⅔ full. Bake until toothpick inserted in center comes out clean, about 25 to 30 minutes. Frost with your favorite icing.

Note: These cupcakes keep for several days in a tightly covered container or may be frozen.

Upside-down Chocolate Cupcakes

MAKES 12 CUPCAKES

¼ cup butter or margarine, melted
½ cup brown sugar, firmly packed
1 tablespoon water
36 to 48 walnut halves
1 cup cake flour, sifted
⅓ cup cocoa
½ teaspoon baking soda
¼ teaspoon salt
¼ cup butter or margarine
¾ cup sugar
1 egg
½ teaspoon vanilla
½ cup water
⅓ cup sweetened condensed milk
½ cup semisweet chocolate chips
1 tablespoon butter

Preheat oven to 350° F. Well grease 12 muffin pan cups.

In small saucepan, combine the ¼ cup melted butter, brown sugar, and the 1 tablespoon water. Simmer 1 minute. Place 3 or 4 walnut halves in each of the prepared muffin pan cups. Spoon cooked mixture over walnuts.

Sift flour, cocoa, soda, and salt together; set aside. Cream ¼ cup butter. Gradually add sugar and continue creaming until light and fluffy. Beat in egg and vanilla. Blend in dry ingredients alternately with the ½ cup water, beginning and ending with dry ingredients.

Fill muffin pan cups ½ full with batter. Bake for 20 to 25 minutes, until surface springs back when gently touched with fingertip. Remove from muffin pan. Let cool inverted on wire racks.

In small saucepan, combine milk and chocolate. Cook over very low flame, stirring constantly, until smooth and thickened, about 10 minutes. Stir in the 1 tablespoon butter; keep warm. Spread on sides of cupcakes.

Mushroom Caps

MAKES 6 TO 8 SERVINGS

- **1 1-layer devils-food cake mix**

Chocolate Glaze
- **¼ cup light corn syrup**
- **2 tablespoons hot water**
- **2 tablespoons butter**
- **1 package (6 ounces) chocolate chips**

Grease and flour 4-ounce mushroom cans or other ovenproof, ridge-free containers.

Prepare cake mix as directed. Fill prepared small cans ⅔ full; bake as instructed for cupcakes. Cool 5 minutes in cans; remove from cans to cool.

Combine corn syrup, water, and butter in a saucepan; bring to a boil. Continue to heat until butter melts. Remove from heat. Stir in chocolate chips until they melt. Cool to room temperature. Place cakes on a rack that is resting on waxed paper. Spoon Chocolate Glaze over cakes until covered. Let glaze set before serving.

English Toffee Refrigerator Cake

MAKES 12 SERVINGS

- **2½ ounces (2½ squares) unsweetened baking chocolate**
- **½ cup milk**
- **⅔ cup granulated sugar**
- **5 egg yolks, beaten**
- **1 cup butter**
- **1 cup confectioners' sugar**
- **5 egg whites**
- **1 cup graham-cracker crumbs**
- **1 cup pecans, chopped**
- **1 cup whipped topping**

Melt chocolate; cool. Combine milk, granulated sugar, and beaten egg yolks in top of double boiler. Cook over boiling water, stirring constantly, until thickened. Cool. Cream butter, powdered sugar, and cooled chocolate together. Blend into cooled egg-yolk mixture. Beat egg whites until stiff. Fold chocolate mixture into egg whites. Blend well.

Combine graham crackers and pecans. Sprinkle half the graham-cracker crumb and nut mixture over the bottom of an 8-inch square pan. Pour chocolate mixture into pan; top with remaining crumb and nut mixture. Chill for 24 hours.

To serve, cut cake into squares. Garnish with whipped topping.

Chocolate Dessert

MAKES 8 TO 10 SERVINGS

- **2 ounces (2 squares) unsweetened baking chocolate**
- **2 cups flour**
- **¼ teaspoon salt**
- **1 teaspoon baking soda**
- **¼ teaspoon bicarbonate of soda**
- **½ cup butter or margarine**
- **¾ cup sugar**
- **2 eggs**
- **1 cup dark beer**
- **½ cup pecans, coarsely chopped**

Filling

- **¼ cup butter, softened**
- **¾ cup confectioners' sugar**
- **1 tablespoon dark beer**
- **2 ounces (2 squares) unsweetened baking chocolate**

Preheat oven to 350° F. Grease and line two 8-inch cake pans. Melt chocolate and let cool.

Sift flour, salt, baking soda, and bicarbonate together. Beat butter and sugar together until light and creamy. Beat in eggs one at a time. Then add melted chocolate and flour mixture alternately with the lager. Beat well. Then fold in pecans.

Put into prepared pans and bake for 25 to 30 minutes. Leave in pans to cool for 5 minutes before turning out.

To make filling: Beat butter and sugar until creamy; add lager and melted chocolate, beat well, and chill until required. Sandwich the cakes with half the filling, and spread the rest on top. Decorate with extra pecans or whipped cream if desired.

French Chocolate Cake

MAKES ABOUT 10 SERVINGS

- **7 ounces semisweet chocolate**
- **14 tablespoons butter or margarine**
- **4 eggs**
- **¾ cup sugar**
- **1 cup flour**
- **⅓ cup hazelnuts, coarsely chopped**
- **1 teaspoon baking powder**

Preheat oven to 425° F. Grease a springform pan with detachable bottom that has a diameter of about 9½ inches.

Melt cooking chocolate and butter in a thick-bottomed pot over low heat. Beat eggs and sugar until light and airy. Carefully stir the somewhat cooled chocolate mixture into egg mixture.

Blend flour, nuts, and baking powder together, and fold carefully into batter. It's important to fold it in gently.

Pour batter into pan and bake in the oven for about 15 minutes. The cake should not become firm. The "unbaked" batter tastes like a delicious filling.

You may garnish cooled cake with a little bit of grated chocolate and a ring of whipped topping.

French Chocolate Cake

Chocolate Cheese Cake

MAKES 12 SERVINGS

- **½ package (6 ounces) chocolate chips**
- **1¼ cups sugar, divided usage**
- **1½ cups graham-cracker crumbs**
- **2 tablespoons sugar**
- **¼ cup butter, melted**
- **2 packages (8 ounces each) cream cheese, softened**
- **½ cup sour cream**
- **1 teaspoon vanilla**
- **4 eggs**

Preheat oven to 325° F. In double boiler over low heat, melt chocolate chips and ½ cup sugar. Set aside.

In small bowl, combine graham-cracker crumbs, 2 tablespoons sugar, and melted butter. Press in a 9-inch springform pan, 1½ inches up sides. In large bowl, beat cream cheese until creamy. Add the remaining ¾ cup sugar. Stir in sour cream and vanilla. Beat in eggs, one at a time, until well blended. Divide batter in half. Stir chocolate into one half.

Pour chocolate batter into pan. Cover with plain batter by spoonfuls. Swirl with a knife. Bake for 50 minutes, or until a 2- to 3-inch circle in center will shake. Cool at room temperature and refrigerate.

Devil's Food Cake

MAKES 8 TO 10 SERVINGS

- **3 ounces (3 squares) unsweetened baking chocolate**
- **1 cup boiling water**
- **2½ cups cake flour, sifted**
- **¼ teaspoon salt**
- **½ cup butter or margarine**
- **2 cups sugar**
- **3 eggs, separated**
- **1 cup dairy sour cream**
- **1 teaspoon vanilla**
- **1¼ teaspoons baking soda**
- **1 teaspoon red food coloring**

Preheat oven to 350° F. Line two 8-inch square pans with greased waxed paper. Set aside.

Break chocolate into pieces. Melt in water; let cool. Sift flour and salt together; set aside. Cream butter. Gradually add 1½ cups of the sugar and continue creaming until light and fluffy. Beat in egg yolks one at a time. Blend in dry ingredients alternately with sour cream and vanilla, beginning and ending with dry ingredients. Dissolve soda in chocolate; stir chocolate mixture and coloring into batter. Beat egg whites until foamy. Gradually add remaining ½ cup sugar and continue beating until soft peaks form; fold into batter.

Pour into prepared pans. Bake until toothpick inserted in center comes out clean, about 40 to 45 minutes. Remove from pans; peel off waxed paper. Let cool on wire racks.

Chocolate Feather Cake

MAKES 8 TO 10 SERVINGS

2½ ounces (2½ squares) unsweetened baking chocolate
2½ cups cake flour, sifted
¼ teaspoon salt
1 cup butter or margarine
2 cups sugar
5 eggs, separated
1 cup buttermilk
1½ teaspoons vanilla
1 teaspoon baking soda
1 tablespoon hot water

Preheat oven to 350° F. Line two 8 × 8 × 2-inch pans with greased waxed paper. Set aside.

In double boiler, melt chocolate; let cool. Sift flour and salt together; set aside. Cream butter or margarine. Gradually add sugar and continue creaming until light and fluffy. Beat in chocolate, then egg yolks one at a time. Blend in dry ingredients alternately with milk and vanilla, beginning and ending with dry ingredients. Beat thoroughly, about 1 minute.

Dissolve soda in water; stir into batter. Beat egg whites until stiff but not dry; fold into batter.

Pour batter into prepared pans. Bake until toothpick inserted in center comes out clean, about 40 to 45 minutes. Remove from pans; peel off waxed paper. Let cool on wire racks.

Easy Chocolate Cake

MAKES ABOUT 16 PIECES

2 ounces (2 squares) unsweetened baking chocolate
½ cup boiling water
1 cup cake flour, sifted
1 cup sugar
¼ teaspoon baking powder
½ teaspoon baking soda
¼ teaspoon salt
¼ cup shortening
½ teaspoon vanilla
1 egg
Confectioners' sugar

Preheat oven to 350° F. Grease and flour an 8-inch square pan.

Melt chocolate in boiling water in medium saucepan over very low heat. Remove from heat; cool. Sift flour, sugar, baking powder, baking soda, and salt together. Stir into chocolate mixture. Add shortening. Beat for 1 minute on medium speed with electric mixer. Add remaining ingredients except confectioners' sugar; beat for 1 more minute.

Pour into prepared pan. Bake for 30 to 35 minutes, or until center of cake springs back when touched lightly. Cool cake; sprinkle with confectioners' sugar.

Almond Mousse Layers

MAKES 6 TO 8 SERVINGS

Cake
- ½ **to ⅔ cup almonds**
- ⅓ **cup sugar**
- 3 **egg whites**

Mocha-Cream Icing
- 5 **ounces semisweet chocolate**
- ¾ **cup heavy cream**
- 2 **tablespoons confectioners' sugar**
- 2 **tablespoons strong coffee, *or***
- 3 **or 4 drops peppermint oil, *or***
- 2 **tablespoons rum**
- 2 **egg yolks**

Garnish
- **Chocolate or roasted slivered almonds**

Preheat oven to 350° F. Cover a cookie sheet with baking paper.

Grind the unskinned almonds. Mix them with sugar. Beat egg whites until stiff. Carefully fold in the almonds and sugar. Spread batter into 2 round "cookies," about 8 inches in diameter, on prepared cookie sheet. Bake in the center of preheated oven until they feel dry and are light brown in color, about 15 minutes. Let them cool somewhat. Loosen them from the paper with a sharp knife.

Break chocolate into pieces. Place in a bowl. Cover with foil. Place bowl over a pan of boiling water. Remove pan from heat and let chocolate melt slowly.

Whip cream, but not too stiffly. Add sugar, flavoring, egg yolks, and 2 tablespoons of cream to the chocolate. Beat vigorously. Let cool. Mix in rest of the cream.

Put layers together with slightly more than half of the icing between layers. Spread rest of the icing on top. Refrigerate cake for at least a couple of hours before serving.

Garnish with chocolate almonds or chocolate curls.

Cherry Chocolate Cake

MAKES 8 TO 10 SERVINGS

- 3 **eggs**
- 1 **can (1 pound, 5 ounces) cherry pie filling**
- 1 **package (about 1 pound, 2 ounces) chocolate, devil's food, or fudge cake mix**

Preheat oven to 350° F. Grease and flour 9-inch bundt pan or 13 × 9 × 2-inch pan.

In bowl, combine eggs, pie filling, and dry cake mix. Using wooden spoon, mix well. Pour into prepared pan. Bake about 35 minutes, until toothpick inserted in center comes out clean. Remove from pan. Let cool on wire rack. Garnish with powdered sugar.

Almond Mousse Layers

Old-fashioned Devil's Food Cake

MAKES 12 TO 14 SERVINGS

3 ounces (3 squares) unsweetened baking chocolate
2 cups all-purpose flour, sifted
2 teaspoons baking soda
¼ teaspoon salt
½ cup (1 stick) butter or margarine
2 cups light brown sugar, firmly packed
3 eggs
1½ teaspoons vanilla
1½ cups milk
1 cup pecans, chopped

Frosting
1 cup (6 ounces) semisweet chocolate chips
½ cup sour cream
1½ teaspoons vanilla
3 cups confectioners' sugar
1 container (10 ounces) whipped topping

Preheat oven to 350° F. Line two 9-inch round cake pans with waxed paper.

In double boiler, melt chocolate over low heat, or melt in microwave oven on HIGH for 1 to 1½ minutes. In medium bowl, sift flour, baking soda, and salt together, mixing well. Set aside. In large bowl, cream butter and sugar. Add eggs one at a time, beating well after each addition. Add vanilla and melted chocolate; beat until light and fluffy. Add dry ingredients a little at a time, alternating with milk; mix well after each addition. Stir in pecans.

Pour into prepared pans. (Batter will be thin.) Bake 25 to 30 minutes, or until a toothpick inserted in center comes out clean. Cool on racks 15 minutes. Remove from pans and cool completely before frosting.

To make frosting, melt chocolate chips over very low heat. Remove from heat and stir in sour cream and vanilla. Gradually beat in confectioners' sugar, until smooth. If too soft to spread, refrigerate ½ hour. Carefully slice each layer in half horizontally. Spread one layer with half the whipped topping; top with second layer, and spread with half the frosting. Repeat layers, spreading remaining frosting on sides of cake. Garnish with chopped pecans. Chill 1 hour.

Fudge Brownie Cake

MAKES 8 TO 10 SERVINGS

2 cups all-purpose flour
½ teaspoon baking soda
½ teaspoon salt
⅓ cup butter or margarine
1 cup sugar
1 egg
1½ teaspoons vanilla
2 ounces (2 squares) unsweetened baking chocolate, melted
1 cup buttermilk
½ cup semisweet chocolate chips
½ cup walnuts, chopped
Fudge Frosting (see Index)

Preheat oven to 350° F. Grease and lightly flour a 9-inch round pan.

Sift flour. Measure and sift again with baking soda and salt. Set aside. In a large bowl, cream butter or margarine and sugar until light and fluffy. Beat in egg and vanilla. Add melted chocolate. Blend in flour alternately with buttermilk, beginning and ending with flour. Beat until smooth. Stir in chocolate chips and nuts.

Pour into prepared pan. Bake on middle oven rack for 45 to 55 minutes. Cool before removing from pan. Frost with Fudge Frosting.

Gypsy John

MAKES 12 SERVINGS

Chocolate Cake

1 cup cake flour
¼ cup unsweetened cocoa
1 teaspoon baking powder
¼ teaspoon salt
3 large eggs
1 cup sugar
⅓ cup water
1 teaspoon vanilla

Chocolate Filling

10 ounces (10 squares) semisweet baking chocolate
2 cups heavy cream
2 tablespoons rum

Chocolate Icing

¼ cup light corn syrup
2 tablespoons hot water
2 tablespoons butter
1 package (6 ounces) semisweet chocolate bits

Preheat oven to 375° F. Line jelly roll pan with waxed paper; grease.

Sift flour, cocoa, baking powder, and salt together twice; set aside. Place eggs in small mixing bowl. Beat with electric mixer 5 minutes or until thick and lemon-colored. Slowly beat in sugar, a tablespoon at a time. Mixture will become very thick. Transfer to large mixing bowl. Beat in water and vanilla. Slowly add flour mixture; beat until smooth. Pour into prepared pan, spreading evenly to corners. Bake 12 to 15 minutes, or until cake tests done. Loosen from pan. Turn out on rack; remove waxed paper. Invert; cool completely.

Combine baking chocolate, broken into pieces, and cream in heavy saucepan. Heat slowly, stirring constantly, until chocolate melts. Transfer to medium-sized mixing bowl. Stir in rum; chill 1 to 2 hours. Beat with electric mixer until stiff and thick. Cut cake in half crosswise. Place 1 piece of cake on small cookie sheet. Top with chocolate filling; spread to form even layer 1½ inches thick. Top with remaining cake layer. Chill at least 1 hour.

Prepare frosting. Combine corn syrup, water, and butter in small saucepan. Bring to boil; cook until butter melts. Remove from heat. Add chocolate bits; stir until chocolate melts. Cool to room temperature. Spread over top of cake. Chill until frosting sets.

Cut cake into 12 squares; arrange on decorative plate.

Mint Chocolate Cake

MAKES ABOUT 8 SERVINGS

2½ ounces (2 squares) unsweetened baking chocolate
5¼ tablespoons butter or margarine
¾ cup sugar
¼ teaspoon vanilla
2 eggs
1 cup flour
1 teaspoon baking powder
⅓ cup cream

Mint Filling
⅓ cup sugar
⅓ cup strong coffee
3 egg yolks
⅔ cup unsalted butter, room temperature
1¾ ounces light cooking chocolate, melted
2 to 3 drops peppermint oil

Preheat oven to 350° F. Heavily grease and flour a 1½-quart pan.

Break baking chocolate into smaller pieces. Melt it in a double boiler.

Mix butter, sugar, and vanilla until airy. Add eggs, one at a time. Beat mixture until smooth. Blend in chocolate.

Mix flour and baking powder together. Add this and the cream to batter. Pour batter into prepared pan. Bake 40 to 50 minutes. Test with a toothpick.

To make mint filling, boil the sugar and coffee together until syrupy. Beat egg yolks lightly. Add sugar and coffee mixture in a thin trickle, stirring constantly and vigorously. Let cool. Add butter in dabs, continuing to beat vigorously. Flavor with melted chocolate and peppermint oil.

Divide cake into 3 layers. Spread mint filling between the layers. Serve cake with cold whipped cream.

Chocolate Angel Food Cake

MAKES 20 SERVINGS

1 cup all-purpose flour
¼ cup cocoa
1½ cups sugar
10 egg whites
1½ teaspoons cream of tartar
⅛ teaspoon salt
1½ teaspoons vanilla

Preheat oven to 325° F.

In medium bowl, sift flour. Sift flour again twice with cocoa and ½ cup sugar. Set aside. In large bowl, beat egg whites, cream of tartar, and salt until soft peaks form. Gradually add remaining sugar, 2 tablespoons at a time, until stiff peaks form. Fold in flour mixture and vanilla.

Pour into ungreased tube pan. Bake for 55 to 65 minutes. Invert pan for about 1 hour, or until cake is cool.

Mint Chocolate Cake

Red Devil's Food Cake

MAKES 8 TO 10 SERVINGS

1¾ cups all-purpose flour, sifted
⅓ cup cocoa
1 tablespoon instant coffee
½ teaspoon salt
1½ cups sugar
½ cup butter or margarine, softened
2 eggs
1½ teaspoons red food coloring
1 teaspoon vanilla
½ cup buttermilk
1½ teaspoons baking soda
¾ cup boiling water

Preheat oven to 350° F. Grease and line two 8-inch pans with waxed paper.

Sift flour, cocoa, instant coffee, and salt together. Set aside. Beat sugar and butter or margarine together until creamy. Beat in eggs, one at a time. Add food coloring and vanilla. Gradually add dry ingredients and buttermilk alternately in small amounts, beating until smooth after each addition. Stir baking soda into boiling water; add and mix smooth.

Pour thin batter into prepared pans, and bake for 30 to 35 minutes. Turn out on rack and peel waxed paper. Frost each layer with your favorite frosting.

Ice Cream Cake with Chocolate Icing

MAKES ABOUT 6 SERVINGS

1 quart vanilla ice cream
½ to ⅔ cup walnuts, chopped
2 to 3 tablespoons white rum, optional
4¼ ounces semisweet chocolate

Garnish
Roasted almonds or pistachio nuts
Candied violets or silver balls, optional

Stir ice cream until soft. Add walnuts and rum. Quickly pour mixture into a form with a detachable edge. Place in freezer to harden.

Melt cooking chocolate over a double boiler.

When ice cream has hardened, release spring on the edge and remove the side of the form. Brush sides and top with a carelessly applied first layer of chocolate. Place ice cream back in freezer without form edge. Let it freeze again for ½ to 1 hour. Take it out of freezer. Brush again with chocolate. None of the ice cream should show through after this brushing. If it does, patch up the spots with more chocolate. Spread out rest of chocolate with a spatula. Sprinkle with garnish before chocolate hardens. Place again in freezer.

Remove ice cream from freezer shortly before it is to be served, but do not detach it from the bottom of dish.

Variations: The ice cream is also tasty when about ½ tablespoon instant coffee is added. The ice cream cake shown in the picture has been made from doubling the recipe.

Buttery Almond Pound Cake

MAKES 12 SERVINGS

½ cup almonds, sliced
3½ cups all-purpose flour
2 teaspoons baking powder
¾ cup butter or margarine
2 cups sugar
2 eggs
1 small can (5 ounces) evaporated milk
½ cup water
1 teaspoon vanilla
Hot Fudge Sauce (see Index) (optional)

Preheat oven to 350° F. Generously grease 10-inch tube pan. Sprinkle sliced almonds into prepared pan, shaking to cover bottom and sides.

Combine flour and baking powder; set aside. In large mixing bowl, cream butter. Gradually add sugar and beat until fluffy. Beat in eggs. Mix in half the flour mixture. Stir in evaporated milk, water, and vanilla. Mix in remaining flour and blend well.

Pour batter into almond-lined pan. Bake 40 to 45 minutes, or until toothpick inserted near center comes out clean. Top individual cake slices with Hot Fudge Sauce, if desired.

Sour Cream Chocolate Cake

MAKES 10 TO 12 SERVINGS

2 cups all-purpose flour, sifted
⅔ cup cocoa
1 teaspoon baking soda
¼ teaspoon salt
⅔ cup butter or margarine, softened
1¾ cups sugar
2 eggs
1 teaspoon vanilla
1 cup sour cream
½ cup milk

Filling
1½ cups confectioners' sugar
½ cup sour cream
¼ cup cocoa
¼ cup butter or margarine
1 container (8 ounces) whipped topping
Slivered almonds, optional

Preheat oven to 350° F. Grease and lightly flour two 8-inch round cake pans.

Sift flour, cocoa, baking soda, and salt together. Set aside. Cream butter and sugar in a large bowl until light and fluffy. Beat in eggs, one at a time; add vanilla and beat until fluffy. Slowly add dry ingredients, mixing well. Blend in sour cream and milk. Mix only until smooth. Pour batter into prepared pans. Bake 25 to 30 minutes. Cool 10 minutes before removing from pans.

Prepare filling by beating all ingredients except whipped topping together until smooth. Fold in whipped topping. Cut each cake layer in half horizontally. Spread filling between cooled cakes. Stack and garnish with slivered almonds if desired.

The Ultimate Chocolate Cake

very good

MAKES 10 TO 12 SERVINGS

2 cups all-purpose flour
⅔ cup cocoa
1½ teaspoons baking soda
¼ teaspoon baking powder
1⅔ cups sugar
4 eggs
1 teaspoon vanilla
1 cup mayonnaise
1⅓ cups water

Preheat oven to 350° F. Grease and flour bottoms of two 9-inch cake pans.

In medium bowl, combine flour, cocoa, soda, and baking powder; set aside. In large bowl, beat sugar, eggs, and vanilla together until light and fluffy. At low speed, beat in mayonnaise. Add flour mixture gradually, alternating with water, beginning and ending with flour.

Pour into prepared pans. Bake for 30 to 35 minutes, or until cakes test done. Allow to cool 10 minutes before removing from pans. Frost with your favorite frosting.

Slightly Frozen Cake

MAKES 6 TO 8 SERVINGS

2 meringue cake layers, bought or homemade
¾ to 1¼ cups whipped cream
½ package orange sherbet

Meringue Layers
3 or 4 egg whites (⅓ cup)
⅔ cup sugar

Chocolate Sauce
¼ cup heavy cream
1½ ounces (1½ squares) unsweetened baking chocolate, broken into pieces

Preheat oven to 300° F.

To make meringue layers, beat egg whites in a clean bowl with a dry, clean beater until they form stiff, dry peaks. Continue to beat for a few more minutes. Sprinkle with sugar. Fold sugar into egg whites with a couple of deep strokes with a spoon.

Draw 2 circles on a piece of baking paper. Spread meringue on the paper within these circles. Bake for about 45 minutes. The meringue is done when it separates from the paper.

Make chocolate sauce by placing heavy cream and chocolate into a saucepan. Heat and stir until chocolate melts and sauce is smooth.

To put cake together, alternate meringue cake layers, chocolate sauce, whipped cream, and sherbet. Grate sherbet over whipped cream, using coarse side of a grater. Repeat with the next layer. Place cake in freezer for an hour or until time to serve it. If it is in the freezer longer than an hour, thaw it some before serving.

If you wish to decorate the cake, make decorations with soft sherbet and a pastry bag.

Slightly Frozen Cake

Chocolate Potato Cake

MAKES 6 SERVINGS

1 medium-sized potato
1½ ounces (1½ squares) semisweet baking chocolate
⅔ cup butter
6 tablespoons sugar
2 eggs
1 teaspoon vanilla
1½ cups flour
1 teaspoon baking powder
½ teaspoon ground cinnamon
¼ teaspoon ground nutmeg
⅛ teaspoon salt
½ cup milk
½ cup hazelnuts, finely chopped

Chocolate-Rum Icing
1 tablespoon egg white
1 cup confectioners' sugar
1 tablespoon cocoa
1½ tablespoons rum

Preheat oven to 350° F. Grease and flour 9 × 5 × 3-inch loaf pan; set aside.

Peel potato; coarsely grate. Place in tea towel and squeeze dry. There should be ¾ cup potato. Set aside. Grate chocolate; set aside. Cream butter and sugar until light. Add eggs and vanilla; beat well. Sift flour, baking powder, spices, and salt together. Add alternately with milk to creamed mixture. Add potato, chocolate, and nuts; mix well.

Turn into prepared loaf pan. Bake 55 minutes, or until cake tests done. Cool cake in pan 30 minutes; turn out onto wire rack.

Beat egg white in small bowl with fork until foamy. Add confectioners' sugar, cocoa, and rum; stir until smooth. Spread over cake while cake is still warm.

Chocolate Pound Cake

MAKES 12 SERVINGS

2¾ cups all-purpose flour
¼ cup unsweetened cocoa
½ teaspoon baking powder
¼ teaspoon salt
2⅔ cups sugar
1½ cups butter or margarine
1½ teaspoons vanilla
4 large eggs
¾ cup milk

Glaze
1 cup confectioners' sugar
1 tablespoon cocoa
1 to 2 tablespoons milk

Preheat oven to 350° F. Grease and lightly flour a 10-inch bundt pan.

Sift flour, cocoa, baking powder, and salt together. Set aside. In large bowl, cream sugar and butter or margarine. Add vanilla and eggs one at a time, beating well after each addition. Add flour mixture and milk, alternately beginning and ending with flour.

Pour into prepared pan. Bake on middle oven rack for 70 to 75 minutes, until toothpick inserted comes out clean. Cool ½ hour before removing from pan.

In small bowl, combine confectioners' sugar, cocoa and milk. Drizzle over top of cake.

Moor In A Shirt

MAKES 4 SERVINGS

4 slices bread, crusts removed
½ cup whipping cream
⅓ cup butter, softened
2 eggs
2 egg yolks
¾ cup confectioners' sugar, sifted
¼ cup toasted almonds, ground
⅓ cup chocolate chips, melted
⅛ teaspoon almond extract

Heavily butter a 1- to 1½-quart pudding mold.

Break bread into small pieces and place in bowl. Pour cream over bread, then mix with wooden spoon until cream is absorbed. Place butter in small mixer bowl and cream with electric mixer for about 5 minutes, or until light and creamy. Add bread mixture and beat until light and fluffy. Combine eggs and egg yolks and beat lightly with fork. Add eggs and sugar alternately to bread mixture, a small amount at a time, beating well after each addition. Add almonds, chocolate, and almond extract and beat until well blended.

Turn into prepared pudding mold. Cover with buttered waxed paper and heavy-duty foil, then tie securely with string. Trim off excess paper and foil. Place on rack in steamer and pour boiling water just to bottom of rack. Cover with lid and steam for 2 hours.

Remove from steamer and let rest for 2 minutes. Unmold onto serving dish and dust with additional confectioners' sugar. Serve with whipped topping or chocolate sauce, if desired.

Tiger Cake

MAKES 10 SERVINGS

2¼ cups flour
2 teaspoons baking powder
⅔ cup butter or margarine
1⅓ cups sugar
3 eggs
⅔ cup cream or milk
1 teaspoon vanilla
2 tablespoons cocoa
1 cup chocolate chips (for glaze)
Sliced almonds or other nuts

Preheat oven to 350° F. Well grease a loaf pan or cake mold.

Measure and sift flour and baking powder and set them aside. Using an electric beater, cream butter and sugar. Add unbeaten eggs one at a time. Add half the flour and half the milk, beating thoroughly after each addition. Add remainder of flour and milk, and vanilla. Set aside a third of the batter in another bowl. Add cocoa to this.

In a prepared pan or cake mold, put alternate layers of light and dark batter, ending with light batter on top. Gently run a long-tined fork through all the cake batter to form a striped pattern. Bake for 50 to 60 minutes. Allow cake to cool completely.

Glaze top of the cake with melted chocolate and sprinkle with nuts.

Steamed Chocolate Pudding

MAKES ABOUT 8 SERVINGS

- **½ cup butter, softened**
- **¾ cup sugar**
- **¾ cup all-purpose flour**
- **3 tablespoons cocoa**
- **⅛ teaspoon salt**
- **3 eggs**
- **½ teaspoon vanilla**
- **¼ cup half-and-half**
- **Confectioners' sugar**

Heavily butter a 1- to 1½-quart metal mold or pyrex dish. Use 1 to 2 tablespoons butter to grease mold.

Cream butter in bowl with electric mixer until light and fluffy. Add sugar and beat for about 5 minutes. Sift flour, cocoa, and salt together. Beat in flour mixture and eggs alternately, beginning and ending with flour mixture. Add vanilla and half-and-half and beat in thoroughly.

Turn into prepared dish. Place a double thickness of buttered waxed paper over top, then cover with a double thickness of heavy-duty foil. Tie this tightly with heavy string. Trim paper and foil, leaving only about 1 inch overhang. If mold has a lid, place on top. Place rack in steamer and add boiling water just to bottom of rack. Place the mold on the rack. Bring to a boil, then cover with lid. Reduce heat to low and cook at a low boil for 2 hours, adding boiling water occasionally to keep water level just below rack.

Remove mold from steamer. Let rest for about 2 minutes, then remove covers and unmold. Dust generously with confectioners' sugar. Serve plain, with whipped cream or chocolate sauce.

Minute Chocolate Cake

MAKES 8 TO 10 SERVINGS

- **½ package chocolate pudding mix**
- **1 cup heavy cream**
- **1 teaspoon instant coffee**
- **1 to 2 tablespoons cocoa**
- **1 meringue cake layer (see below)**
- **⅔ cup whipped cream**
- **Cocoa**
- **Chocolate thins**

Mix chocolate-pudding powder with heavy cream. Add instant coffee and cocoa to create a fuller taste. Adjust flavoring.

Immediately spread the pudding icing over the meringue cake. Spread a layer of whipped cream on top of this. Sift over with the cocoa. Press chocolate thins into whipped topping. Refrigerate cake before serving.

To make meringue layer: Beat 2 egg whites with electric mixer until soft peaks form. Gradually add ¼ cup sugar, beating until stiff peaks form. Spread meringue (not too thinly) on cookie sheet lined with baking paper. Bake at 300° F for 30 to 35 minutes. Allow to cool.

Minute Chocolate Cake

Sachertorte

MAKES ABOUT 16 SERVINGS

- **8 eggs**
- **6 ounces (6 squares) semisweet baking chocolate**
- **¾ cup butter or margarine**
- **¾ cup sugar**
- **1 teaspoon vanilla**
- **1 cup cake flour, sifted**
- **⅛ teaspoon cream of tartar**
- **½ cup apricot preserves, heated and mashed with fork**

European Chocolate Icing

- **2 squares semisweet baking chocolate**
- **2 squares unsweetened baking chocolate**
- **1⅓ cups confectioners' sugar, sifted**
- **3 tablespoons whipping cream (approximately)**

Preheat oven to 275° F. Line bottom of 9-inch springform pan with greased waxed paper.

Separate 7 of the eggs; leave 1 egg whole; set aside. In double boiler, melt chocolate; let cool slightly. Using medium speed on mixer, cream butter. Gradually add ½ cup of the sugar and continue creaming until light and fluffy. Mix in vanilla, then chocolate.

Beat in egg yolks one at a time, then whole egg. Using low speed, blend in flour. Using high speed with clean beaters and separate bowl, whip egg whites until frothy. Add cream of tartar and continue beating until soft peaks form when beater is slowly raised. Gradually add remaining sugar and continue beating until stiff peaks form. Fold into chocolate mixture.

Pour into prepared pan. Bake about 1⅓ hours, until toothpick inserted in center comes out clean. Let cool slightly. Remove sides of pan. Let cool completely. Halve horizontally. Spread preserves evenly on bottom half of torte. Frost with European Chocolate Icing.

To make icing, melt chocolates in double boiler. Beat in sugar and cream alternately until smooth and of spreading consistency.

Quick Petits Fours

MAKES 32 SERVINGS

- **1 8-inch loaf angel food cake**

Chocolate Topping

- **2 containers (10 ounces each) whipped topping**
- **2 tablespoons sugar**
- **1 tablespoon cocoa**
- **1 cup angel-flake coconut**

Cut cake into 2-inch squares. Blend whipped topping, sugar, and cocoa. Roll cake squares in Chocolate Topping; sprinkle with coconut.

Chocolate Tea Cakes

MAKES 32 CAKES

1 10-inch square yellow-cake layer

Chocolate Glaze
½ cup light corn syrup
⅓ cup hot water
4 tablespoons margarine
1 package (12 ounces) chocolate chips

Cut cake into 2-inch strips. Cut each strip into 4 equal pieces. Cut each piece into 2 triangles.

Combine corn syrup, water, and margarine in saucepan; bring to boil. Continue to heat until butter melts. Remove from heat. Stir in chocolate chips until they melt. Cool to room temperature.

Place each cake triangle onto a 2-prong frying fork. Spoon cooled chocolate glaze over cakes until well covered. Place on cooling rack to allow excess chocolate to drip from cakes.

Muscat Chocolate Dutch Cake

MAKES 8 TO 12 SERVINGS

1½ cups seeded raisins
½ cup walnuts
2 ounces (2 squares) unsweetened baking chocolate, chopped
1 teaspoon instant coffee
1 cup boiling water
½ cup butter, softened
1¾ cups brown sugar, firmly packed
2 teaspoons vanilla
2 eggs, well beaten
2 cups flour, sifted
1¼ teaspoons salt
1 teaspoon soda
1 teaspoon cinnamon
½ cup dairy sour cream

Preheat oven to 325° F. Grease and flour a bundt pan.

Chop raisins and nuts. Dissolve chocolate and instant coffee in boiling water. Beat butter with half of sugar until light. Beat in remaining sugar and vanilla until fluffy. Thoroughly mix in eggs. Stir in raisins, walnuts, and chocolate liquid. Resift flour with salt, soda, and cinnamon. Add flour mixture alternately with sour cream; stir only until blended.

Turn into prepared bundt pan. Bake for 50 minutes, or until cake tests done. Remove from pan and cool on rack. Sift powdered sugar over top, if desired.

Cocoa Spice Cake

MAKES 8 TO 10 SERVINGS

1½ cups flour
4 tablespoons cocoa
1 teaspoon cinnamon
½ cup shortening
1¼ cups sugar
1 egg, beaten
1 cup buttermilk
1 teaspoon baking soda
1 teaspoon vanilla

Preheat oven to 350° F. Grease two 9-inch round pans. Set aside.

In medium bowl, combine flour, cocoa, and cinnamon. Set aside. In large bowl, cream shortening and sugar. Add egg and beat until light and fluffy. Gradually add flour mixture, alternating with buttermilk (into which the 1 teaspoon of baking soda has been stirred). Mix well. Stir in vanilla.

Pour into prepared pans. Bake for 30 to 35 minutes. Remove from oven and cool 10 minutes before removing from pans. Frost with your favorite frosting.

Macaroon Cake

MAKES 6 SERVINGS

2 cups almond paste
2 eggs

Chocolate-Cream Filling
1⅔ cups whipping cream
3 tablespoons confectioners' sugar
3 tablespoons cocoa
3 tablespoons strong, cold coffee

Decoration
Roasted sliced almonds
Tiny, candied pearls (optional)

Preheat oven to 400° F. Well grease baking paper and sprinkle it with flour.

Finely grate marzipan with grater. Mix it with eggs. Stir into smooth batter. Spread it out into 4 thin, round "cookie" layers, about 7 inches in diameter, on prepared baking paper. Bake for 8 to 10 minutes, or until layers have become golden brown. Let them become cold on a flat surface.

To make filling, whip the cream. Stir in confectioners' sugar, cocoa, and coffee, which both have first been sifted. Adjust flavoring.

Place cake layers together with filling in between and on top. Sprinkle with almonds and candied pearls. Refrigerate cake overnight or for several hours before it is to be served.

Macaroon Cake

Coffee Cakes and Breads

Chocolate Upside-down Cake

MAKES 12 TO 14 SERVINGS

½ cup butter or margarine, melted
¼ cup water
1 cup brown sugar
1 cup chopped nuts
1⅓ cups flaked coconut
1 package (18½ ounces) chocolate cake mix

Preheat oven to 350° F. Grease 13 × 9 × 2-inch pan with melted butter or margarine.

In small bowl, combine water, brown sugar, nuts, and coconut. Spread evenly in pan. Set aside. In medium bowl, prepare cake mix according to package directions. Pour batter over brown sugar mixture.

Bake for 40 to 45 minutes. Remove from oven and let cool about 5 minutes, until topping begins to set. Turn upside down onto a large platter.

Chocolate Spice Cake

MAKES 12 TO 14 SERVINGS

1 package (1 pound, 2 ounces) chocolate cake mix
1 cup buttermilk
½ teaspoon baking soda, dissolved in buttermilk
1 can (16 ounces) applesauce
1 cup (6 ounces) semisweet chocolate chips
½ cup walnuts, chopped
¼ cup sugar

Preheat oven to 350° F. Grease and lightly flour a 9 × 13 × 2-inch pan.

In large bowl, combine cake mix, buttermilk, baking soda, and applesauce until smooth. Pour into prepared pan. In small bowl, combine chocolate chips, nuts, and sugar. Sprinkle on top of cake. Bake for 40 to 45 minutes.

Chocolate Coffee Cake

MAKES 10 TO 12 SERVINGS

- **2 cups (12 ounces) semisweet chocolate chips, divided usage**
- **1 package (8 ounces) cream cheese, softened**
- **¼ cup sugar**
- **1 cup plus 2 tablespoons milk**
- **3 cups all-purpose flour**
- **½ cup brown sugar**
- **1 teaspoon baking soda**
- **1 teaspoon baking powder**
- **¾ cup butter or margarine**
- **2 eggs, slightly beaten**
- **1½ teaspoons vanilla**

Crumb Topping

- **½ cup all-purpose flour**
- **¼ cup brown sugar**
- **¼ cup sugar**
- **¼ cup butter or margarine**
- **½ cup pecans, chopped**

Preheat oven to 350° F.

Grease a 13 × 9 × 2-inch pan. Set aside.

In double boiler over low heat, melt chocolate; cool. Combine cream cheese, sugar, and 2 tablespoons milk in small bowl. Stir in melted chocolate; set aside. In large bowl, combine flour, brown sugar, baking soda, and baking powder. Cut in butter or margarine until mixture resembles fine crumbs. In small bowl, combine eggs, remaining 1 cup milk and vanilla. Stir in flour mixture just to moisten. Spread half the batter into prepared pan. Top with chocolate mixture, spreading evenly. Spoon remaining batter over top.

To make Crumb Topping, combine flour and sugars in small bowl. Cut in butter or margarine. Stir in pecans. Sprinkle topping over cake. Bake at 350° F for 40 to 45 minutes on middle oven rack. Cool slightly before cutting.

Chocolate Chip Coffee Cake

MAKES 10 TO 12 SERVINGS

- **Fine bread crumbs**
- **½ pound butter or margarine**
- **1 cup sugar**
- **2 eggs**
- **2 cups flour, sifted**
- **1 teaspoon baking powder**
- **1 teaspoon baking soda**
- **½ pint sour cream**
- **1 teaspoon vanilla**
- **½ cup chocolate chips**
- **½ cup brown sugar**
- **½ cup nuts, chopped**
- **1 teaspoon cinnamon**

Preheat oven to 350° F. Grease a 10-inch tube pan and coat it with bread crumbs.

Cream butter and sugar. Beat in eggs until fluffy. Sift flour, baking powder, and baking soda; add alternately with sour cream to creamed mixture. Stir in vanilla and chocolate chips.

Spoon evenly into prepared pan. Combine brown sugar, nuts, and cinnamon; press on top of batter. Bake 45 minutes, or until toothpick inserted in center comes out clean.

Marbled Chocolate Loaf

MAKES 6 SERVINGS

- **⅓ cup shortening**
- **1 cup sugar**
- **1 teaspoon vanilla**
- **2 cups cake flour**
- **1½ teaspoons baking powder**
- **¼ teaspoon salt**
- **⅔ cup milk**
- **3 egg whites**
- **1 ounce (1 square) baking chocolate**
- **2 tablespoons hot water**
- **¼ baking soda**

Preheat oven to 350° F. Grease and line a 9×5×3-inch loaf pan.

Beat shortening and sugar until light and fluffy. Add vanilla.

Sift flour, baking powder, and salt together; add to creamed mixture alternately with milk. Beat well with each addition. Beat egg whites stiffly and fold into mixture. Mix melted chocolate with water and baking soda. Add this mixture to half the cake batter.

Alternate light and dark batters by spoonfuls in prepared loaf pan. Then bake for 40 to 45 minutes.

When cold, frost with your favorite frosting.

Fudgy Applesauce Cake

MAKES 9 SERVINGS

- **⅓ cup shortening**
- **1 cup sugar**
- **2 eggs**
- **1 cup flour, unsifted**
- **⅓ cup cocoa**
- **½ teaspoon baking soda**
- **½ teaspoon salt**
- **1 teaspoon allspice**
- **½ cup nuts, chopped**
- **1 cup applesauce**
- **¼ cup milk**

Preheat oven to 350° F. Grease a 9×9×2-inch baking pan.

Beat shortening and sugar together until creamy; beat in eggs. Mix dry ingredients thoroughly. Add nuts. Add dry ingredients, applesauce, and milk to creamy mixture. Stir only until mixed.

Pour into baking pan. Bake 45 to 50 minutes, or until surface is firm when touched lightly. Cool before cutting.

Marbled Chocolate Loaf

Chips and More Muffins

MAKES 12 LARGE MUFFINS

- **2 cups all-purpose flour**
- **6 tablespoons brown sugar, firmly packed**
- **1 tablespoon baking powder**
- **1 teaspoon salt**
- **1 cup milk**
- **6 tablespoons butter or margarine, melted**
- **1 egg**
- **1 cup (6 ounces) semisweet chocolate chips**
- **½ cup pecans, chopped**

Preheat oven to 375° F. Grease muffin tins.

In large bowl, combine flour, sugar, baking powder, and salt. In separate bowl, beat milk, butter, and egg together. Pour liquid into dry ingredients and mix just until moistened. Stir in chocolate chips and pecans.

Spoon into prepared muffin tins. Bake 25 minutes or until golden brown.

Note: Muffins may be individually wrapped and frozen. They can be reheated in the microwave on 50% POWER or DEFROST for 50 to 70 seconds, or until warm.

Chocolate Peach Muffins

MAKES 16 MUFFINS

- **1¾ cups all-purpose flour**
- **¼ cup sugar**
- **1½ teaspoons baking powder**
- **¾ cup milk**
- **¼ cup vegetable oil**
- **1 egg**
- **1 cup dried peaches, chopped**
- **1 cup pecans, chopped**
- **1 package (6 ounces) semisweet chocolate chips**
- **¼ cup raisins (optional)**

Preheat oven to 400°F. Grease muffin pans. In medium bowl, combine flour, sugar, and baking powder. Set aside.

In large bowl, blend milk, vegetable oil, and egg. Add flour mixture, mixing well. Stir in dried peaches, pecans, and chocolate chips. Spoon into prepared pans, filling each about ¾ full. Bake for 18 to 20 minutes. Allow to cool for 5 minutes before removing from pans.

Chocolate Rich Crescent Croissants

MAKES 8 CRESCENTS

1 can (8 ounces) refrigerated crescent rolls
2 tablespoons margarine or butter, softened
4 ounces sweet baking chocolate
¼ cup sugar
1 teaspoon cinnamon
½ cup confectioners' sugar
2 to 3 teaspoons milk

Preheat oven to 375°F.

Separate dough into 8 triangles; spread with margarine. Break chocolate into 8 equal pieces. Place chocolate on shortest side of each triangle. In small bowl, combine sugar and cinnamon. Sprinkle 1½ teaspoons sugar over each triangle. Roll up dough, at shortest point. Place on ungreased cookie sheet, point side down. Curve into crescent shape.

Bake for 11 to 13 minutes, or until golden brown. Combine confectioners' sugar and milk. Drizzle over crescents.

Banana Chocolate Chip Bread

MAKES 6 SERVINGS

2 cups flour, sifted
1 teaspoon baking powder
½ teaspoon baking soda
1 cup sugar
1 egg
½ cup butter or margarine
1 cup bananas, mashed
3 tablespoons milk
1 cup (8 ounces) semisweet chocolate chips

Preheat oven to 350°F. Well grease 9×5×3-inch loaf pan.

In medium bowl, sift flour, baking powder, and baking soda together; set aside. Cream sugar, egg, and butter until light and fluffy. Blend in bananas and milk. Add dry ingredients just until moistened. Stir in chocolate chips.

Pour into prepared pan. Bake for 1 hour, or until toothpick comes out clean. Cool in pan for 10 minutes before removing.

Pies

Fudge Pecan Pie

MAKES 8 SERVINGS

- **1 frozen 9-inch, deep-dish pie crust shell**
- **½ cup butter**
- **3 tablespoons cocoa**
- **¾ cup hot water**
- **2 cups sugar**
- **½ cup flour**
- **⅛ teaspoon salt**
- **1 teaspoon vanilla**
- **⅔ cup milk**
- **1 cup pecan halves**
- **1 cup whipped topping, thawed**

Preheat oven and cookie sheet to 350°F.

In medium saucepan, melt butter. Add cocoa and stir until dissolved. Add hot water and stir again. With wire whisk blend in sugar, flour, salt, vanilla, and milk. Stir until batter is smooth. Mix in pecans and pour into pie crust. Bake on preheated cookie sheet for 50 minutes, or until custard sets. Remove from oven and allow to cool for at least 1½ to 2 hours. Garnish with whipped topping.

S'more Pie

MAKES 8 SERVINGS

- **1 graham cracker crust pie shell**
- **1 cup peanuts, chopped**
- **¼ cup semisweet chocolate chips**
- **1 cup miniature marshmallows, halved**
- **1 quart chocolate ice cream**
- **2 tablespoons chocolate syrup**

In small mixing bowl, combine peanuts, chocolate chips, and marshmallows. Set aside.

Scoop ⅓ of the ice cream into graham crust. Gently smooth ice cream with a rubber spatula. Sprinkle ½ of peanut mixture on top of ice cream layer. Layer with another ⅓ of ice cream. Sprinkle remaining peanut mixture over layer. Top with remaining ⅓ of ice cream. Swirl chocolate syrup over top of pie. Freeze until firm, about 4 hours. Remove pie from freezer about 10 minutes before serving.

Fudge Pecan Pie

Frozen Milk Chocolate Pie

MAKES 8 SERVINGS

- **1 frozen 9-inch pie crust shell, baked**
- **3 ounces (3 squares) semisweet chocolate**
- **⅔ cup milk**
- **2 cups miniature marshmallows**
- **⅓ cup almonds, chopped and toasted***
- **½ teaspoon almond extract**
- **1 container (10 ounces) whipped topping**
- **Maraschino cherries**

Bake pie shell, following directions on package. Set aside.

Melt chocolate in 2-quart saucepan. Add milk to melted chocolate and heat, stirring until combined. Mix in marshmallows, stirring constantly until melted. Stir in almonds. Transfer to a 2-quart bowl; refrigerate until cool, about 20 to 30 minutes, stirring twice. Add almond extract; fold in whipped topping.

Spoon into baked pie shell. Freeze several hours, until firm. Remove from freezer 10 minutes before serving. If desired, garnish with additional whipped topping, chopped almonds, and maraschino cherries.

* To toast almonds: Place almonds on cookie sheet in 350°F oven, stirring occasionally until almonds are lightly toasted, about 10 minutes.

Black Bottom Cake Pie

MAKES 8 SERVINGS

- **1 frozen 9-inch deep dish pie crust shell**
- **1½ cups sugar, divided usage**
- **⅓ cup cocoa**
- **¾ cup milk, divided usage**
- **1 teaspoon vanilla, divided usage**
- **⅓ cup pecans, chopped**
- **¼ cup butter or margarine, softened**
- **1 egg, beaten**
- **1 cup flour**
- **1 teaspoon baking powder**
- **whipped topping, thawed**
- **Chocolate syrup**

Preheat oven to 350° F.

Combine ½ cup sugar, cocoa, ¼ cup milk, ½ teaspoon vanilla, and pecans; set aside. Beat butter or margarine and 1 cup sugar until creamy. Beat in egg and remaining ½ teaspoon vanilla. Blend flour and baking powder together. Add flour mixture and milk to butter mixture; blend well.

Spread cocoa mixture over bottom of unbaked pie crust shell. Spread butter mixture evenly over cocoa mixture. Bake on baking sheet for 40 to 45 minutes, or until a wooden toothpick inserted near center comes out clean. Cool. Serve with whipped topping and chocolate syrup, if desired.

Brandied Black Bottom Pie

MAKES 6 SERVINGS

Crust
- 2 cups gingersnaps
- 1/4 cup butter, softened
- 1/4 cup sugar

Filling
- 4 eggs, separated
- 1/2 cup dark brown sugar
- 1 1/4 tablespoons cornstarch
- 1/4 teaspoon salt
- 1 1/2 cups milk, scalded
- 6 tablespoons brandy, divided usage
- 2 ounces (2 squares) unsweetened baking chocolate, melted
- 1 teaspoon vanilla
- 1 envelope gelatin
- 2 tablespoons cold water
- 1/4 teaspoon cream of tartar
- 1/2 cup sugar
- whipped topping
- Shaved chocolate

Make crust: Roll cookies to fine crumbs. Blend crumbs with butter and sugar. Press into bottom and sides of pie pan.

Beat egg yolks until light. Put in double boiler. Sift brown sugar, cornstarch, and salt together and add. Gradually stir in scalded milk. Add 5 tablespoons brandy. Cook over hot water until thick and smooth, stirring constantly. Remove from hot water. Stir the melted chocolate and vanilla into 1 1/2 cups of the custard. Let cool and pour into the pie shell.

To rest of hot custard, add gelatin softened in 2 tablespoons of cold water and remaining 1 tablespoon brandy, mixing well. Cool mixture slightly, but do not allow to set. Beat egg whites stiffly with cream of tartar. Beat in 1/2 cup sugar. Fold into warm custard. Pour this over the chocolate custard. Chill at least 4 hours.

To serve, spread pie with whipped topping. Sprinkle with shaved sweet chocolate.

Brownie Pie I

MAKES 8 SERVINGS

- 1 frozen 9-inch pie crust shell
- 4 ounces (4 squares) semisweet chocolate
- 1/2 cup butter or margarine
- 3/4 cup brown sugar, firmly packed
- 1/4 cup water
- 2 eggs, separated
- 1 teaspoon vanilla
- 1/3 cup all-purpose flour
- 1/4 teaspoon salt
- 3/4 cup pecans, chopped

Preheat oven and cookie sheet to 350°F.

In medium saucepan, melt chocolate and butter. Cool slightly. In small mixing bowl, combine brown sugar, water, egg yolks, and vanilla. Stir into chocolate mixture. Fold in flour and salt. Beat egg whites until stiff; fold into chocolate mixture. Stir in pecans.

Spread in pie shell. Bake on preheated cookie sheet about 30 minutes. Cool completely.

Brownie Pie II

MAKES 6 TO 8 SERVINGS

- **1 frozen 9-inch pie crust shell**
- **2 ounces (2 squares) unsweeetened baking chocolate**
- **2 tablespoons butter or margarine**
- **3 eggs, well beaten**
- **¾ cup dark corn syrup**
- **½ cup sugar**
- **¼ teaspoon salt**
- **¾ cup walnuts, chopped**

Preheat oven to 375°F.

In large saucepan, melt chocolate and butter together. Let cool. Add eggs, syrup, sugar, and salt. Using rotary beater, beat thoroughly. Stir in walnuts.

Pour into pie shell. Bake until set for 50 to 60 minutes. Serve slightly warm or cold.

Fudge Brownie Pie

MAKES 8 SERVINGS

- **1 frozen 9-inch, deep-dish pie crust shell**
- **½ cup butter or margarine**
- **1½ ounces (1½ squares) unsweetened baking chocolate**
- **1 cup brown sugar, firmly packed**
- **½ cup sugar**
- **¼ cup flour**
- **2 eggs**
- **2 tablespoons milk**
- **1 teaspoon vanilla**
- **whipped topping, thawed**

Preheat oven to 400°F. Thaw pie crust 10 minutes. Prick bottom and sides thoroughly with fork. Bake on baking sheet 8 minutes or until partially baked. Cool. Reduce heat to 325°F.

Melt butter or margarine and chocolate over medium heat in saucepan. Remove from heat. Combine brown sugar, sugar, and flour. Stir into chocolate mixture. Beat in eggs, milk, and vanilla. Pour into pie shell.

Bake on baking sheet, at 325°F, 50 minutes or until set. Cool. Serve with whipped topping.

Chocolate Cake Pie

MAKES 8 SERVINGS

- **1 frozen 9-inch, deep-dish pie crust shell**
- **1½ cups sugar, divided usage**
- **⅓ cup cocoa**
- **¾ cup milk, divided usage**
- **1 teaspoon vanilla, divided usage**
- **⅓ cup pecans, coarsely chopped**
- **1 cup flour, sifted**
- **1 teaspoon baking powder**
- **¼ cup butter or margarine, softened**
- **1 egg, slightly beaten**
- **whipped topping, thawed**
- **Chocolate syrup**

Preheat oven and cookie sheet to 350°F.

Mix together ½ cup of sugar, cocoa, ¼ cup of milk, ½ teaspoon vanilla and nuts. Set aside. Meanwhile, mix butter and remaining sugar together until blended. Beat in egg and remaining vanilla. Sift flour and baking powder together; add to creamed mixture along with remaining milk. Spread chocolate mixture into bottom of pie shell. Spread batter over cocoa mixture.

Bake on preheated cookie sheet until toothpick inserted comes out clean, about 40 to 45 minutes. Cool completely. Just before serving, spread top with whipped topping and drizzle with chocolate syrup.

Chocolate Cheesecake Pie

MAKES 8 SERVINGS

- **1 frozen 9-inch, deep-dish pie crust shell**
- **4 packages (3 ounces each) cream cheese, softened**
- **½ cup sugar**
- **2 eggs**
- **1 cup sour cream**
- **2 ounces (2 squares) semisweet baking chocolate**

Chocolate Glaze

- **1 ounce (1 square) semisweet baking chocolate**
- **1 tablespoon sugar**
- **1 tablespoon butter or margarine**
- **¼ cup milk**

Preheat oven and cookie sheet to 400°F. Thaw pie shell for 10 minutes. Prick bottom and sides with fork. Partially bake for 8 minutes. Cool slightly. Reduce oven temperature to 375°F.

Beat cream cheese and sugar together. Add eggs, one at a time, beating after each addition. Blend in sour cream. In double boiler, melt 2 ounces of chocolate over medium heat. Stir into cream cheese mixture. Pour into pie shell. In double boiler, prepare Chocolate Glaze: combine remaining 1 ounce chocolate, sugar, butter or margarine, and milk. Stir constantly over medium heat until smooth and creamy. Spread evenly over pie. Refrigerate at least 3 hours. Serve with Strawberry Sauce.

Strawberry Sauce

- **1 pint strawberries, washed, hulled, and sliced**
- **¼ cup sugar**
- **1 tablespoon cornstarch**
- **½ cup water**

To make Strawberry Sauce: Combine sugar, cornstarch, and water in a small saucepan. Stir until dissolved. Add strawberries and cook over medium heat until strawberries are soft and mixture is thickened and bubbly. Chill. To serve, spoon strawberry sauce over wedges of pie.

Fudge Sundae Pie

MAKES 8 TO 10 SERVINGS

- **1 cup milk**
- **1 cup (6 ounces) semisweet chocolate chips**
- **¼ teaspoon salt**
- **1 cup miniature marshmallows**
- **30 vanilla wafers**
- **4 cups vanilla ice cream, softened**
- **Almond halves**

In heavy saucepan, combine milk, chocolate chips, and salt. Stir over low heat until chocolate melts completely and mixture thickens. Remove from heat and add marshmallows. Stir rapidly until marshmallows melt and mixture is smooth. Cool to room temperature.

Line bottom and sides of 9-inch pie pan with vanilla wafers. Spread half the ice cream over wafers. Cover with half the chocolate mixture. Repeat with remaining ice cream and chocolate. Garnish with almonds. Freeze at least 5 hours, or until firm.

Heavenly Pie (Chocolate Angel Pie)

MAKES 8 SERVINGS

Meringue Shell

- **1 cup sugar**
- **¼ teaspoon cream of tartar**
- **¾ cup nuts, chopped, optional**
- **4 egg whites**

Filling

- **6 ounces sweet chocolate**
- **1 teaspoon vanilla**
- **3 tablespoons hot water**
- **1 pint whipping cream**

Preheat oven to 275°F for meringue. Beat egg whites until stiff. Slowly add sugar and cream of tartar, sifted. Put in 9- or 10-inch pie pan, making bottom ¼ inch thick and sides 1 inch high. Bake for 1 hour and 15 minutes, until barely brown. Nuts may be added to the meringue before cooking.

To make filling, melt chocolate and stir in hot water. Cook until thick. Cool. Add vanilla and fold in half the cream, whipped. Put into cooled meringue shell and cover with other half of cream, whipped. Refrigerate from 12 to 24 hours.

Note: Try adding 2 teaspoons instant coffee to filling for variation.

Chocolate Mousse Pie

MAKES 8 SERVINGS

- **1 frozen 9-inch pie crust shell**
- **½ cup butter, softened**
- **¾ cup sugar**
- **2 ounces (2 squares) unsweetened baking chocolate, melted and cooled**
- **1 teaspoon vanilla**
- **2 eggs**
- **1 tablespoon orange liqueur, optional**
- **whipped topping**
- **Strawberries**

Preheat oven and cookie sheet to 400°F. Remove pie crust from freezer; let thaw 10 minutes. Prick bottom and sides of pie crust with fork. Bake on preheated cookie sheet for 12 minutes or until golden brown. Let cool.

In medium bowl, cream butter. Gradually beat in sugar and continue beating until light and fluffy. Blend in chocolate and vanilla. Add eggs, one at a time, beating 3 minutes after each addition. Stir in orange liqueur.

Spoon into cooled pie crust. Chill for 4 hours. Just before serving, garnish with whipped topping and strawberries.

Chocolate Silk Pie

MAKES 8 SERVINGS

- **1 frozen 9-inch pie crust shell**
- **½ cup butter or margarine, softened**
- **¾ cup sugar**
- **2 ounces (2 squares) unsweetened baking chocolate, melted**
- **1 teaspoon vanilla**
- **2 eggs**
- **1½ cups whipped topping, thawed**
- **2 tablespoons pecans, finely chopped**

Bake pie shell according to package directions for empty baked crust. Cool thoroughly.

Beat butter or margarine until smooth and creamy. Gradually beat in sugar until fluffy. Blend in chocolate and vanilla. Beat in eggs, one at a time, beating 3 minutes after each addition.

Spread filling in baked pie shell. Chill 2 hours or until firm. Just before serving, spread whipped topping over chilled filling. Sprinkle pecans over pie.

Chocolate-covered Peanut Pie

MAKES 8 SERVINGS

- **1 graham cracker crust pie shell**
- **1 quart vanilla ice cream, softened**
- **1 cup whipped topping**
- **½ cup peanut butter**
- **1 cup peanuts, chopped**
- **1 recipe Hot Fudge Sauce (see below)**

Combine ice cream, whipped topping, peanut butter, and ½ cup peanuts. Mix thoroughly. Spoon into graham cracker shell. Top with remaining peanuts. Freeze until firm, several hours or overnight. Serve with Hot Fudge Sauce.

Hot Fudge Sauce

- **1 cup (6 ounces) semisweet chocolate chips**
- **¾ cup milk**
- **¼ cup sugar**

Combine all ingredients in heavy saucepan. Stir over low heat until chocolate melts completely. Cool. Makes 1 cup.

Chocolate Marshmallow Pie

MAKES 8 SERVINGS

- **1 frozen 9-inch pie shell, baked, or 1 home-baked pastry pie shell**
- **2 ounces (2 squares) unsweetened baking chocolate**
- **2 tablespoons sugar**
- **½ cup milk**
- **12 marshmallows**
- **1 (10-ounce) container whipped topping, thawed**
- **½ cup toasted almonds, chopped**

Put chocolate, sugar, milk, and marshmallows into top of double boiler. Stir over hot water until melted. Let cool, stirring frequently.

Fold whipped topping into chocolate mixture. Pour into pastry shell, sprinkle with almonds, and chill thoroughly before serving.

Chocolate Marshmallow Pie

Cocoa Cheese Pie

MAKES 8 SERVINGS

- **18 graham crackers, finely crushed (about 1⅓ cup crumbs)**
- **¼ cup butter, softened**
- **1 cup sugar, divided usage**
- **1 envelope unflavored gelatin**
- **¼ cup cold water**
- **¾ cup boiling water**
- **1 cup cream-style cottage cheese**
- **½ cup commercial sour cream**
- **⅓ cup unsweetened cocoa**

Preheat oven to 375°F. Thoroughly stir crackers, butter, and ¼ cup of the sugar together. Press firmly against bottom and sides of a 9-inch pie plate. Bake 8 minutes; cool.

In a blender, sprinkle gelatin over cold water. Let stand until gelatin swells, about 5 minutes. Add boiling water and process on low speed about 2 minutes. Add remaining ¾ cup sugar, the cottage cheese, sour cream, and cocoa; process on high speed until smooth.

Pour into prepared crust. Chill 4 hours or overnight.

Coffee Liqueur Pie

MAKES 8 SERVINGS

- **1 frozen 9-inch pie crust shell, baked**
- **⅔ cup milk**
- **½ cup (3 ounces) semisweet chocolate chips**
- **2 cups miniature marshmallows**
- **⅓ cup toasted almonds, chopped***
- **⅓ cup coffee liqueur**
- **1 container (10 ounces) whipped topping, thawed**
- **Maraschino cherries, optional**

Prepare pie shell. Set aside.

In heavy 1-quart saucepan, combine milk and chocolate chips. Cook over low heat, stirring occasionally, until chocolate melts completely and mixture thickens. Stir in marshmallows until melted. Remove from heat. Add almonds. Pour into 2-quart bowl and refrigerate 20 to 30 minutes or until cool, stirring twice.

Add coffee liqueur. Fold in whipped topping. Spoon into baked shell. Freeze several hours or until firm. Remove from freezer 10 minutes before serving for ease in cutting. Garnish with additional whipped topping, chopped almonds, and maraschino cherries if desired.

* To toast almonds: Place almonds on baking sheet in preheated 350°F oven and bake about 10 minutes, or until almonds are lightly toasted, stirring frequently.

Chocolate Crunch Ice Cream Pie

MAKES 6 TO 8 SERVINGS

- **½ cup (3 ounces) semisweet chocolate chips**
- **3 tablespoons butter or margarine**
- **2 cups oven-toasted rice cereal**
- **1 quart ice cream**
- **Shaved chocolate**

In medium saucepan, melt chocolate pieces and butter together. Add cereal. Stir to coat cereal thoroughly. Press on bottom and sides of buttered 9-inch pie pan. Chill until crust is firm. Fill with ice cream. Garnish with shaved chocolate, if desired. Serve immediately, or freeze until ready to use.

Chocolate Mint Pie Surprise

MAKES 8 SERVINGS

- **1 frozen 9-inch, deep-dish pie crust shell**
- **⅓ cup semisweet chocolate chips, melted**
- **2 eggs, separated, at room temperature, divided usage**
- **¼ cup sugar**
- **2 tablespoons Creme de Menthe or ¼ teaspoon peppermint extract**
- **⅛ teaspoon green food coloring**
- **1 container (10 ounces) whipped topping, thawed**
- **Shaved chocolate**

Prepare pie shell following directions on package. Spread melted chocolate on sides and bottom of crust. Chill. Beat egg whites until soft peaks form. Gradually beat in sugar until stiff peaks form. In large bowl, beat egg yolks with Creme de Menthe and food coloring. Blend in whipped topping. Fold in beaten egg whites.

Spread filling in crust. Garnish with shaved chocolate. Freeze until firm, about 3 hours.

Candies

Heavenly Hash ✓

MAKES ABOUT 3 DOZEN LARGE PIECES

- **1 package (12 ounces) semisweet chocolate chips**
- **1 can (14 ounces) sweetened condensed milk**
- **1 package (10½ ounces) miniature marshmallows**
- **1 cup pecan halves or pieces**

In double boiler, melt chocolate over medium heat. Stir until smooth and creamy. Remove from burner. Slowly blend in milk. Add marshmallows and pecans. Mix until marshmallows and pecans are well coated with chocolate.

Drop by tablespoonfuls onto greased cookie sheets. Refrigerate until firm.

Fudge Nut Log

MAKES ABOUT 3 DOZEN SLICES

- **1 cup brown sugar, firmly packed**
- **¼ cup light corn syrup**
- **¼ cup milk**
- **1½ teaspoons vanilla**
- **1 cup (6 ounces) semisweet chocolate chips**
- **3 cups pecans, chopped, divided usage**

Combine sugar, syrup, and milk in 1½-quart saucepan. Bring to full boil, stirring constantly for 2 to 3 minutes. Remove from heat. Beat in vanilla. Add chocolate chips and 1½ cups pecans. Stir until chocolate melts. Beat with wire whisk until smooth.

Divide chocolate mixture in half and form 2 logs. Roll each log separately in remaining chopped nuts. Wrap logs in waxed paper. Refrigerate until firm, about 2½ to 3 hours. To serve, cut logs into ½-inch slices.

Heavenly Hash

Brandy Balls

MAKES 4 DOZEN

- 1 **cup (6 ounces) semisweet chocolate chips**
- 1 **small can (5 ounces) evaporated milk**
- 2½ **cups cookie crumbs**
- ½ **cup confectioners' sugar, sifted**
- 1 **cup pecans, coarsely chopped**
- ⅓ **cup brandy**

Combine chocolate chips and milk in 2-quart saucepan. Cook over low heat, stirring constantly, just until chocolate is melted and mixture well blended. Remove from heat.

Combine remaining ingredients; add to melted-chocolate mixture, mixing well. Cool about ½ hour. Shape mixture into small balls about 1 inch in diameter. Finished balls can be rolled in confectioners' sugar, cocoa, candy sprinkles, ground nuts, or flaked coconut. For a very pretty tray of brandy balls, use a variety of coatings. Let finished brandy balls air-dry an hour or two, then store in airtight container in refrigerator. Be sure to bring to room temperature before serving.

Variation: Raisin-Rum Balls. Soak ½ cup seedless raisins in ⅓ cup rum; drain well. Use rum in place of brandy in recipe as directed. Form balls with several raisins in center. If you want a shortcut, just mix raisins right into other ingredients.

Classic Hazelnut Chocolate Squares ✓

MAKES 128 SQUARES

- 1 **recipe Canache (see Index)**
- 1 **package (12 ounces) semisweet chocolate bits**
- 1 **cup roasted hazelnuts (also called filberts), finely chopped**
- ¾ **cup sweetened condensed milk**
- 1 **teaspoon vanilla**

Prepare Canache; chill in 8 × 8 × 2-inch pan.

While Canache is cooling, melt chocolate bits over hot, not boiling, water. Remove from heat; add nuts, milk, and vanilla. Beat gently with wooden spoon until completely blended and slightly thickened.

Spread carefully over cooled Canache. Chill in refrigerator until completely cold and set. Cut with very sharp knife into ½-inch squares. Store in airtight container in very cool place. They will keep very well if kept cold, since this truffle contains no egg yolks.

Variation: Basic Hazelnut Truffle. Prepare only the chocolate-hazelnut mixture (above). After mixture cools enough so it can be handled easily, it may be formed into ½-inch balls and rolled in your favorite coating. A delicious way to vary the coating is to roll truffle ball first in melted chocolate, then, while chocolate is still moist, roll it again in cocoa to coat.

Baked Chocolate Marshmallow Treats

MAKES 1 DOZEN TREATS

- **6 graham crackers, halved**
- **3 milk chocolate candy bars**
- **6 large marshmallows, halved**

Preheat oven to 500° F.

Place cracker halves on ungreased cookie sheets. Top each half with two 1-inch squares chocolate. Add marshmallow half on top of chocolate. Bake until marshmallow toasts, about 2 minutes. Serve open-faced. This can also be served sandwich style covered with another cracker half.

Canache

MAKES 100 ½-INCH BALLS

- **1 package (12 ounces) chocolate chips, melted**
- **¾ cup whipping cream**

Melt chocolate chips over hot, not boiling, water.

Heat cream in double boiler until bubbling steadily. Gradually pour cream into melted chocolate, beating vigorously with wooden spoon until dark and glossy. Return chocolate mixture to double boiler. Cook over medium heat, stirring frequently, about 25 minutes or until mixture is thick and falls heavily from spoon. Cool 5 minutes.

Spread quickly in well-oiled 8 × 8 × 2-inch pan. Chill about 2 hours or until mixture is firm enough to handle easily. Cut candy into small squares or triangles, or use canapé cutters and cut into fancy, interesting shapes. You can also break off small pieces and form into ½-inch balls, which can be rolled in ground nuts, chocolate jimmies, cocoa, or any coating that may strike your fancy.

Rum Balls

MAKES 3 DOZEN BALLS

- **1 cup cookie crumbs, chocolate or vanilla**
- **1 cup confectioners' sugar**
- **1½ cups walnuts, finely chopped**
- **2 tablespoons light corn syrup**
- **4 tablespoons rum**
- **2 tablespoons cocoa**

Combine cookie crumbs, sugar, 1 cup walnuts, corn syrup, rum, and cocoa; mix well. Form into 1-inch balls. Roll each ball in reserved walnuts. Air-dry about 1 hour. Store in airtight container in cool place. Will keep several weeks.

Variations: Garnish each finished ball with ½ candied cherry or ½ walnut pressed into top. Or reduce nuts to 1 cup. Roll finished balls in sugar or shredded coconut.

Almond Toffee Candy

MAKES 1¼ POUNDS

1 cup almonds, slivered
1 stick (½ cup) butter
1 cup sugar
½ teaspoon salt
¼ cup milk
¾ cup semisweet chocolate chips

Place almonds on well-greased baking sheet to form a 10 × 7-inch rectangle. Combine butter, sugar, salt, and milk in small saucepan. Bring to boil; reduce heat and simmer 20 minutes, or until mixture turns to a light brown color. Pour mixture over almonds. Let cool.

Melt chocolate in double boiler. Spread chocolate evenly over toffee mixture. Freeze until firm. Break into pieces.

Chocolate Nuggets ✓

MAKES 4 TO 5 DOZEN NUGGETS

1 cup (6 ounces) semisweet chocolate chips
⅔ cup milk
2½ cups graham cracker crumbs
½ cup confectioners' sugar
½ cup pecans, chopped
1 teaspoon rum or almond extract or 3 tablespoons of your favorite liqueur
¾ cup pecans, very finely chopped, *or*
½ cup confectioners' sugar, sifted

In heavy saucepan, combine chocolate chips and milk over very low heat until chocolate melts completely. Remove from heat. Stir in graham cracker crumbs, ½ cup sugar, pecans, and extract or liqueur. Let stand at room temperature 30 minutes.

Form mixture into ½- to 1-inch balls. Roll balls in pecans or ½ cup sifted powdered sugar. Chill at least 1 hour.

Peanut Butter/Chocolate Fudge ✓

MAKES 64 PIECES

¼ cup peanut butter
¾ cup milk
16 large marshmallows
1 cup sugar
½ teaspoon salt
1 cup (6 ounces) semisweet chocolate chips
½ cup salted peanuts, chopped

In 2-quart heavy saucepan, combine peanut butter, milk, marshmallows, sugar, and salt. Stir continuously over low heat until marshmallows melt and mixture is well blended. Bring to a boil and let boil for 5 minutes.

Remove from heat and add chocolate chips. Stir until chips are completely melted. Add peanuts and mix well. Pour into a buttered 8 × 8-inch pan. Let cool completely and cut into 1-inch squares.

Chocolate Nuggets, Peanut Butter/Chocolate Fudge, Almond Toffee Candy

Fudge

MAKES 64 SQUARES

2 ounces (2 squares) unsweetened baking chocolate
1 cup milk
3 cups sugar
1 tablespoon corn syrup
2 tablespoons butter, softened
1 teaspoon vanilla
½ cup walnuts, chopped, optional

Butter sides of heavy 3-quart saucepan. Combine chocolate, milk, sugar, and corn syrup in saucepan. Heat and stir over medium heat until chocolate melts and sugar dissolves. Cook to 236° F (soft ball). Remove from heat. Cool, undisturbed, until pot is cool to touch.

Add butter, vanilla and nuts. Beat vigorously until fudge stiffens and loses its gloss. Quickly spread into buttered 8-inch square pan. When cool, cut into 1-inch squares.

Fabulous Fudge

MAKES 30 PIECES

2¼ cups sugar
¾ cup milk
16 large marshmallows or 1 cup marshmallow creme
¼ cup butter or margarine
¼ teaspoon salt
1 cup (6 ounces) semisweet chocolate chips
1 teaspoon vanilla
1 cup nuts, cut up, optional

Mix sugar, milk, marshmallows, butter or margarine, and salt in heavy medium saucepan. Cook, stirring constantly, over medium heat to a full boil. Boil and stir 5 minutes. Stir in chocolate until completely melted. Add vanilla and nuts.

Spread in buttered 8-inch square pan. Cool. Cut into 30 pieces.

Double Layer Fudge

MAKES ABOUT 50 PIECES

2¼ cups sugar
¾ cup milk
2 cups miniature marshmallows
¼ cup butter or margarine
½ cup semisweet chocolate chips
½ cup butterscotch pieces

Combine sugar, milk, marshmallows, and butter in medium saucepan. Cook and stir over medium heat until mixture boils. Boil and stir for 5 minutes. Mix half of milk mixture with chocolate chips. Pour into buttered 9-inch loaf pan.

Mix remaining milk mixture with butterscotch pieces. Pour over chocolate mixture. Chill until firm. Cut into pieces.

Note: One-half cup peanut butter may be substituted for butterscotch pieces.

Famous Creamy Marshmallow Fudge

MAKES 64 SQUARES

2 cups sugar
⅔ cup milk
16 large marshmallows
¼ teaspoon salt
1 cup (6 ounces) semisweet chocolate chips
½ cup nuts, chopped, optional
¼ cup butter
1 teaspoon vanilla

Butter bottom and sides of 9-inch square pan. In heavy saucepan, combine sugar, milk, marshmallows, and salt. Heat mixture over medium heat until boiling, stirring constantly. When bubbles cover entire surface, continue to boil 5 additional minutes, stirring constantly.

Remove from heat and beat in chocolate chips, nuts if desired, butter, and vanilla. Continue to beat until chocolate is completely melted. Spread mixture into buttered pan. Chill until firm. Keep refrigerated until ready to serve.

Five Minute Fudge ✓

MAKES ABOUT 100 PIECES

¾ cup butter or margarine, divided usage
1 cup cocoa
4½ cups sugar
1 jar (7 ounces) marshmallow creme
1½ cups milk
2 teaspoons vanilla
1 cup pecans, coarsely chopped

Spray a 13 × 9 × 2-inch pan with vegetable spray. Set aside.

In heavy saucepan sprayed with vegetable spray, melt ½ cup butter. Blend in cocoa until smooth. Add sugar, marshmallow creme, milk, and ¼ cup butter. Cook, stirring constantly, over medium heat until mixture comes to a boil; cook and stir 5 minutes. → Longer

Remove from heat and stir in vanilla. Allow to cool 15–20 minutes. Beat with wooden spoon 1 minute. Blend in nuts. Spread in prepared pan. Cool until set. Cut into 1-inch squares. Store in airtight container in a cool dry place.

Truffles

MAKES 50 BALLS

3 ounces (3 squares) unsweetened baking chocolate
1¼ cups confectioners' sugar, sifted
⅓ cup margarine
3 egg yolks
1 teaspoon vanilla
Melted chocolate, cocoa, ground nuts, chocolate jimmies, or coconut

Melt 3 chocolate squares over hot, not boiling, water.

Meanwhile, combine sugar and margarine in mixing bowl; cream together. Add egg yolks one at a time; blend well after each addition. Stir in the 3 ounces chocolate squares and vanilla. Chill mixture until firm enough to handle easily.

Break off small pieces, form into ½-inch balls. Roll in your favorite coating. (You can use several different coatings and arrange finished truffles in very pretty pattern on serving dish.) Allow finished balls to dry and firm on baking sheet about an hour before storing in airtight container in very cool place. These keep about a week.

If you prefer a square truffle, pour warm mixture into well-oiled 8 × 8 × 2-inch pan. Allow to cool thoroughly. Using very sharp knife, cut cooled chocolate into small squares. Coat finished squares with unsweetened powdered cocoa. An easy way to do this is to use an ordinary tea strainer as a sifter. Fill it half full with cocoa; sift very carefully over truffles. Shake off excess cocoa. If you do this on a large piece of wax paper, you can save and reuse the cocoa.

Creamy French Fudge

MAKES 2 POUNDS, 4 OUNCES FUDGE

⅔ cup milk
3 cups confectioners' sugar
1½ packages semisweet chocolate chips
¼ cup butter or margarine
1 teaspoon vanilla

In 2-quart saucepan, combine milk and sugar. Cook over medium heat to a full boil. Remove from heat. Stir in chocolate chips, butter, and vanilla until chocolate melts completely. Spread into buttered 9-inch square pan. Chill until firm. Cut into squares.

Microwave Directions: Combine milk, sugar, and butter in 2-quart microwave dish. Cook on HIGH for 8 minutes, stirring occasionally. Stir in chocolate chips and vanilla until chocolate is completely melted. Spread into buttered 9-inch square pan. Chill until firm. Cut into squares.

Truffles

Creamy Fudge

MAKES 6 DOZEN PIECES

1 cup butter
1 cup cocoa
1 cup milk
2 pounds (7½ cups) confectioners' sugar, sifted
½ teaspoon salt
2 tablespoons vanilla
1 cup pecans or peanuts, chopped
Vegetable spray

In large 4-quart saucepan, melt butter. Add cocoa and blend well. Stir in milk. Gradually mix in sugar and salt until smooth and creamy. Add vanilla and nuts. Stir until well blended.

Pour into 13 × 9 × 2-inch pan sprayed with vegetable spray. Spread evenly. Refrigerate until cool and firm, about 1 hour, or freeze for 20 minutes. Cut into squares.

Chocolate Popcorn Crunch

MAKES 1½ QUARTS POPCORN CRUNCH

⅔ cup brown sugar, firmly packed
½ cup butter or margarine
1 package (12 ounces) semisweet chocolate chips
3 cups freshly popped corn
1 cup plain natural cereal

In large saucepan, melt brown sugar and butter. Cook, stirring constantly about 5 minutes or until thickened. Add chocolate chips and continue stirring until melted. Stir in popcorn and cereal. Cook over low heat until all popcorn is well coated.

Spread onto greased jelly-roll pan one layer deep. Let cool. Break into pieces.

Chocolate Topped Candy

MAKES 3 DOZEN CANDIES

3½ cups confectioners' sugar
⅔ cup milk, divided usage
3 cups natural cereal, any variety
½ package (6 ounces) semisweet chocolate chips

Mix sugar and ⅓ cup of the milk together until smooth. Stir in cereal. Drop by tablespoonfuls onto waxed paper. Heat together remaining milk and chocolate chips just until chocolate melts. Remove from heat. Swirl chocolate on top of each cereal candy. Chill.

Holiday Clusters

MAKES 30 CLUSTERS

1 cup sugar
⅔ cup milk
1 cup (6 ounces) semisweet chocolate chips
1 tablespoon butter or margarine
1 cup natural cereal, any variety

In saucepan, combine sugar and milk. Bring to full boil. Heat and stir 2 additional minutes. Remove from heat. Stir in chocolate chips and butter until chocolate is completely melted. Stir in cereal.

Drop by teaspoonfuls onto waxed paper. Chill until firm.

Nut Toffee Crunch

MAKES 81 SQUARES

1 cup almonds, lightly roasted, coarsely ground, or chopped
1 cup unsalted butter
1 cup sugar
½ cup light brown sugar, firmly packed
3 tablespoons water
½ teaspoon baking soda
1 cup semisweet chocolate chips or 6 (1-ounce) squares semisweet cooking chocolate, melted

Oil 9 × 9 × 2-inch pan very well. Sprinkle ½ cup almonds over bottom of pan.

Melt butter in 2-quart saucepan over low heat. Be very careful not to scorch butter. Add sugars and water. Stirring constantly, cook over low heat until sugars are completely dissolved. Let mixture come to boil. Clip on candy thermometer. Boil, stirring frequently, until thermometer registers a little more than soft-crack stage (280° F).

Remove from heat. Add baking soda, stirring rapidly to blend in completely. Pour over almonds in pan; cool for a minute or two. Sprinkle chocolate bits over hot syrup; use spatula to spread chocolate as it melts from heat of syrup. If you use melted cooking chocolate, allow toffee to cool about 5 minutes, then spread melted chocolate over surface. While chocolate is still warm, sprinkle rest of nuts over surface; press down lightly.

Mark 1-inch squares with edge of sharp knife while toffee is still warm. When completely cooled, break into 1-inch squares along marked lines. Store in airtight container in cool place for indefinite keeping.

Deluxe Topping: For an extra-special treat that turns plain ice cream into a party dessert, try crushing some Nut-Toffee Crunch (well cooled) in blender or food processor. Sprinkle over your favorite ice cream.

Turtles

MAKES 2½ DOZEN

1 cup milk
¼ cup butter
1 cup sugar
1 cup dark corn syrup
¼ teaspoon salt
1 teaspoon vanilla
Whole pecans
½ package (6 ounces) semisweet chocolate chips

In small saucepan, heat butter and milk until butter is melted. In separate 2-quart saucepan, cook sugar, corn syrup, and salt over medium heat, stirring often, until it reaches firm-ball stage (244°F). Slowly stir in hot milk mixture so that sugar mixture does not stop boiling. Stirring constantly, cook mixture until candy reaches firm-ball stage again.

Remove pan from heat and stir in vanilla. Cool caramel to room temperature. On waxed paper, arrange 4 pecans per turtle and place 1 heaping teaspoon of cooled caramel on each. Let cool until firm. Melt semisweet chocolate pieces on top of double boiler. Spread chocolate on top to cover caramel. Let cool until hardened.

Chocolate Candies

MAKES 30 LARGE OR 50 SMALL CANDIES

1¾ cups confectioners' sugar
1⅓ cups cocoa
5¼ tablespoons butter, softened
⅓ cup heavy cream
1½ tablespoons brandy
7 to 9 ounces dark baking chocolate

Sift confectioners' sugar and cocoa together into a bowl. Crumble butter into mixture as much as possible. Add cream and brandy. Mix well, using an electric beater. At first, the mixture will seem impossibly dry, but after awhile it will turn into a smooth dough. Refrigerate for several hours. Roll the chocolate into balls and refrigerate again.

Melt cooking chocolate over a barely simmering double boiler. Roll the chocolate balls in the melted chocolate, using 2 forks. Place the balls on waxed paper and let the chocolate harden. This process has even better results if the balls are placed in a net while the chocolate is hardening.

Those who wish to skip the cooking chocolate can roll the balls in cocoa. This is a classic way of making truffle candy.

Note: It is best to make these candies a week in advance. The proportions given in the recipe are important, so it is best not to double the recipe. Instead, make one batch at a time.

Chocolate Candies

Cookies

Brownies

MAKES 20 SMALL BROWNIES

- **2 ounces (2 squares) unsweetened baking chocolate**
- **½ cup butter or margarine, softened**
- **¾ cup sugar**
- **¼ cup corn syrup**
- **2 large eggs**
- **⅔ cup all-purpose flour**
- **½ cup pecans, chopped**

Preheat oven to 350° F. Butter an 8-inch square cake pan and set aside.

Melt chocolate and butter or margarine in top of a double boiler over low heat. Stir until smooth. Remove from heat. In medium bowl, cream melted chocolate with sugar and corn syrup, about 3 minutes. Beat in eggs one at a time. Fold in flour and pecans, just until blended.

Pour into prepared pan. Bake 20 to 25 minutes; brownies will pull away from sides of pan. Cool in pan before cutting.

Chewy Chocolate Brownies

MAKES ABOUT 40 BROWNIES

- **4 ounces (4 squares) unsweetened baking chocolate**
- **¾ cup butter or margarine**
- **2 teaspoons vanilla**
- **2 cups sugar**
- **4 eggs**
- **1½ cups all-purpose flour, sifted**
- **1 cup pecans, chopped**

Preheat oven to 375° F. Butter a 12 × 8-inch pan.

Melt chocolate with butter over low heat, stirring constantly; or melt in microwave on HIGH for 1 to 1½ minutes. Remove from heat and stir in vanilla. Set aside. In large bowl, cream sugar and eggs about 5 to 6 minutes until sugar is dissolved. Fold chocolate, flour, and nuts into sugar mixture, just until well blended.

Pour into prepared pan. Bake for 25 to 35 minutes. Cool. Frost with your favorite frosting. Refrigerate about 1 hour; cut into squares. Garnish with pecans if desired. Store in refrigerator.

Chocolate Caramel Brownies

MAKES ABOUT 25 BROWNIES

¼ cup butter or margarine
2 ounces (2 squares) unsweetened baking chocolate
2 eggs
1 cup sugar
½ cup all-purpose flour
1 teaspoon salt
½ teaspoon vanilla
½ cup pecan halves, set aside

Caramel Sauce
¼ cup butter or margarine
⅓ cup brown sugar
¾ cup (4 ounces) semisweet chocolate chips, set aside

Preheat oven to 350° F. Lightly grease an 8-inch square pan.

In small saucepan, melt ¼ cup butter or margarine and chocolate over low heat. Set aside. In medium bowl, beat eggs until light. Beat in sugar, flour, salt, and vanilla until blended. Stir in melted chocolate mixture; pour batter into prepared pan. Bake for 15 minutes.

Meanwhile, prepare Caramel Sauce. In small saucepan, mix butter or margarine and brown sugar. Bring to boil, stirring constantly. Stir and simmer 1 minute. Remove brownies from oven and sprinkle evenly with pecans. Gently pour Caramel Sauce over brownies.

Return pan to oven and bake 15 minutes longer, until caramel is bubbling. Remove brownies from oven and sprinkle with chocolate chips. As chocolate chips begin to melt, gently swirl with a knife. Cool completely before cutting. Chill to harden chocolate, if necessary.

Chocolate Chip Brownies

MAKES ABOUT 50 BROWNIES

3 ounces (3 squares) unsweetened baking chocolate
½ cup butter or margarine, softened
1 cup sugar
¾ cup brown sugar, firmly packed
¼ cup milk
3 large eggs
¾ cup all-purpose flour
1 cup semisweet chocolate chips
Confectioners' sugar, optional

Preheat oven to 375° F. Butter and lightly flour a 9 × 13-inch pan. Set aside.

In double boiler over low heat, melt chocolate. Stir until smooth; remove from heat. Cream butter and sugars in large bowl until light and fluffy. Blend in milk. Beat in eggs, one at a time, until well blended. Stir in melted chocolate. Fold in flour and chocolate chips, just until moistened.

Pour into prepared pan. Bake 25 to 30 minutes. Cool in pan before cutting into squares. Dust with confectioners' sugar, if desired.

Cream Cheese Brownies

MAKES 16 SQUARES

- **1 package sweet baking chocolate**
- **5 tablespoons butter**
- **1 package (3 ounces) cream cheese**
- **1 cup sugar**
- **3 eggs**
- **1 tablespoon flour**
- **1½ teaspoons vanilla**
- **½ teaspoon baking powder**
- **¼ teaspoon salt**
- **½ cup flour, unsifted**
- **½ cup nuts, chopped**
- **¼ teaspoon almond extract**

Preheat oven to 350° F. Grease an 8- or 9-inch square pan.

Melt chocolate with 3 tablespoons butter over low heat, stirring constantly. Cool. Cream remaining butter with cream cheese. Gradually add ¼ cup sugar; cream well after each addition. Blend in 1 egg, 1 tablespoon flour, and ½ teaspoon vanilla. Set aside. Beat 2 eggs until thick and light in color. Gradually add ¾ cup sugar, beating until thickened. Add baking powder, salt, and ½ cup flour. Blend in chocolate mixture, nuts, 1 teaspoon vanilla, and almond extract.

Spread about ½ of chocolate mixture in greased pan. Spread cheese mixture over top; spoon on remaining chocolate batter. Zigzag through batters with spatula to marbleize. Bake for 35 to 40 minutes. Cool, then cut into squares.

Marble Brownies

MAKES 16 BROWNIES

- **¼ cup butter or margarine**
- **1 cup sugar**
- **2 eggs**
- **⅔ cup cake flour**
- **¼ teaspoon salt**
- **½ cup nuts, chopped**
- **½ teaspoon vanilla**
- **2 ounces (2 squares) semisweet baking chocolate**

Preheat oven to 350° F. Grease an 8-inch baking pan.

Cream butter; add sugar and beat until light and fluffy. Add eggs and beat until mixture is smooth. Gradually add flour and salt sifted together. Then stir in nuts and vanilla.

Pour half the batter into prepared pan. Mix melted chocolate with the other half, pour over the plain batter, and swirl it through with a spoon. Bake for 30 minutes; cool. Mark into squares or bars and cut when cold.

Marble Brownies

Fudge Brownies

MAKES 25 SQUARES

- **1 cup all-purpose flour**
- **½ teaspoon baking powder**
- **¼ teaspoon salt**
- **⅓ cup cocoa**
- **⅓ cup shortening, softened**
- **1 cup sugar**
- **1 egg**
- **¼ cup milk**
- **½ cup walnuts, chopped**

Preheat oven to 350° F. Grease an 8-inch square baking pan.

Stir flour, baking powder, salt, and cocoa together. In large bowl, cream shortening, sugar, and egg until light and fluffy. Add milk. Gradually mix in flour mixture. Stir in walnuts. Spread in greased pan. Bake for 25 to 30 minutes, or until top springs back when touched lightly with finger. Cut into squares while warm. Cool in pan.

Apple Fudge Squares

MAKES ABOUT 16 SQUARES

- **1 cup all-purpose flour, sifted**
- **½ teaspoon baking powder**
- **¼ teaspoon baking soda**
- **¼ teaspoon salt**
- **½ cup butter or margarine**
- **2 ounces (2 squares) unsweetened baking chocolate**
- **1 cup sugar**
- **⅔ cup applesauce**
- **2 eggs**
- **1 teaspoon vanilla**
- **½ cup pecans, chopped**

Preheat oven to 350° F. Grease an 8-inch square pan on bottom.

Sift flour, baking powder, soda, and salt together; set aside. In double boiler, melt butter and chocolate together over medium heat. Remove from heat and add sugar and applesauce. Beat in eggs one at a time. Blend in vanilla and dry ingredients; stir in pecans.

Pour into prepared pan. Spread evenly. Bake 35 to 40 minutes, until done as desired. Let cool. Cut into squares or bars.

Congo Bars

MAKES 18 BARS

- **⅓ cup butter or margarine**
- **1¼ cups brown sugar, firmly packed**
- **1⅓ cups all-purpose flour**
- **1 teaspoon baking powder**
- **¼ teaspoon salt**
- **½ cup semisweet chocolate chips**
- **½ cup pecans, chopped**
- **1 egg**
- **⅔ cup milk**

Preheat oven to 350° F. Grease and flour a 9-inch square baking pan.

Melt butter in 3-quart saucepan. Remove from heat. Stir in sugar. Allow to cool slightly. Meanwhile, combine flour, baking powder, salt, chocolate pieces, and nuts. Stir egg into cooled sugar mixture. Slowly stir in milk. Add flour mixture, ¼ at a time, mixing well after each addition.

Spread into prepared pan. Bake for 30 minutes, or until lightly browned and cake tester comes out clean. Cool before cutting into bars.

Chocolate Nut Bars

MAKES 32 BARS

1½ cups all-purpose flour
⅔ cup cocoa
¼ teaspoon salt
2 eggs
2 cups sugar
½ cup margarine, melted
⅔ cup milk
2 teaspoons vanilla
1 cup nuts, coarsely chopped

Preheat oven to 350° F. Grease a 13 × 9 × 2-inch baking pan.

Stir flour, cocoa, and salt together. Beat eggs. Gradually add sugar. Stir in melted margarine, milk, and vanilla. Stir in flour mixture. Mix until smooth. Fold in nuts.

Pour into prepared baking pan. Bake for 30 minutes, or until firm to touch. Remove from oven. Let stand 30 minutes before cutting into bars.

Peanut Butter Brownies

MAKES 25 BROWNIES

½ cup cornflake crumbs
¼ teaspoon baking powder
¼ teaspoon salt
½ cup nuts, coarsely chopped
¼ cup margarine or butter
2 ounces (2 squares) unsweetened baking chocolate
1 cup sugar
¼ cup peanut butter
2 eggs, slightly beaten
Confectioners' sugar

Preheat oven to 350° F. Grease a 9 × 9 × 2-inch baking pan.

Mix cornflake crumbs with baking powder, salt, and nuts. Set aside. Melt margarine and chocolate together in medium-sized saucepan over very low heat, stirring constantly. Remove from heat. Add granulated sugar and peanut butter. Stir until well combined. Add eggs. Beat well. Stir in crumbs mixture.

Spread in prepared pan. Bake about 30 minutes, or until wooden pick inserted near center comes out clean. When cool, sift confectioners' sugar over top. Cut into 1¾-inch squares.

Chocolate Chip Bars

MAKES ABOUT 28 BARS

- **2¼ cups all-purpose flour, sifted**
- **1 teaspoon baking soda**
- **½ teaspoon salt**
- **1 cup butter or margarine**
- **¾ cup brown sugar, firmly packed**
- **¾ cup sugar**
- **2 eggs**
- **1½ teaspoons vanilla**
- **1 cup pecans, chopped**
- **1 package (12 ounces) semisweet chocolate chips**

Preheat oven to 375° F. Grease a 15 × 10 × 1-inch jelly roll pan.

Sift flour, soda, and salt together. Set aside. Cream butter. Blend in sugars slowly and continue beating until light and fluffy. Beat in eggs and vanilla. Gradually add dry ingredients. Stir in nuts and chips.

Spread evenly in prepared pan. Bake for 20 to 25 minutes, or until golden brown. Let cool. Cut into 2-inch bars.

Chocolate Filled Bars

MAKES ABOUT 5½ DOZEN BARS

- **2 cups graham-cracker crumbs (about 2 dozen)**
- **¼ cup confectioners' sugar, sifted**
- **½ cup butter or margarine**
- **2 cans (3½ ounces each) flaked coconut**
- **1 can (14 ounces) sweetened condensed milk**
- **1 bar (4 ounces) German's sweet chocolate**
- **2 tablespoons butter or margarine**

Preheat oven to 350° F. Grease 13 × 9 × 2-inch pan.

Combine crumbs and sugar. In medium saucepan, melt ½ cup butter. Add crumb mixture. Stir to coat crumbs thoroughly. Press on bottom of prepared pan. Bake for 10 minutes. Let cool slightly.

Combine coconut and milk. Pour over baked crust. Spread evenly and continue baking until very lightly brown, about 20 minutes. Let cool.

Melt chocolate and remaining butter together in double boiler over medium heat. Pour over coconut filling. Spread evenly. Cut into bars.

Easy Chocolate Chip Bars

MAKES 2 DOZEN BARS

3 cups fine graham cracker crumbs
1 cup sugar
1 cup milk
½ package (6 ounces) semisweet chocolate chips
½ cup pecans, chopped
¼ cup (½ stick) butter or margarine, softened (soften by letting stand at room temperature for 1 hour or microwave on HIGH for 15 to 30 seconds)

Preheat oven to 350° F. Grease 13 × 9 × 2-inch baking dish.

In large bowl, combine all ingredients. Mix well. Spread the mixture in the baking dish. Bake for 30 minutes, or until bar pulls from side of pan. Let cool. Cut into 2-inch bars.

Dream Bars

MAKES 30 BARS

⅓ cup shortening, softened
1½ cups brown sugar, firmly packed
5 tablespoons milk
1 cup plus 2 tablespoons all-purpose flour
1 egg
¼ teaspoon salt
1 teaspoon baking powder
1 teaspoon vanilla
1⅓ cups (3½ ounces) shredded coconut
½ package (6 ounces) semisweet chocolate chips
½ cup pecans, chopped

Preheat oven to 325°F. Grease a 13 × 9 × 1½-inch pan.

Beat shortening, ½ cup brown sugar, and 2 tablespoons milk together until light and fluffy. Gradually mix in 1 cup flour. Press evenly over bottom of prepared pan. Bake for 15 minutes.

Meanwhile, beat egg until foamy. Mix in 1 cup brown sugar, salt, baking powder, 3 tablespoons milk, and vanilla. Stir in coconut, chocolate pieces, pecans, and 2 tablespoons flour. Using 2 forks, spread on baked dough. Bake 30 minutes, or until top is brown. Cut into bars.

Easy No-mix Bar Cookies

MAKES 4 DOZEN BARS

- **¾ cup butter or margarine**
- **2 cups graham cracker crumbs**
- **1 cup (6 ounces) semisweet chocolate chips**
- **1 cup (6 ounces) butterscotch flavored pieces**
- **1 cup pecans, chopped**
- **1½ cups shredded coconut**
- **1 small can (5 ounces) evaporated milk**

Preheat oven to 350°.

Melt butter in 13 × 9-inch baking pan. Sprinkle graham-cracker crumbs over butter in pan. Press down gently. Next layer chocolate pieces, butterscotch pieces, pecans, and coconut. Pour evaporated milk over all. Bake for 30 minutes, or until coconut is lightly browned. Cool. Cut into bars. Cover tightly and refrigerate.

Fancy Layer Cookies

MAKES 32 BARS

- **1¾ cups all-purpose flour**
- **1 teaspoon salt**
- **¼ teaspoon baking soda**
- **¾ cup butter or margarine, softened**
- **1 cup sugar**
- **2 eggs**
- **⅔ cup milk, divided usage**
- **1½ teaspoons vanilla, divided usage**
- **1 ounce (1 square) unsweetened baking chocolate, melted**
- **⅔ cup almonds, coarsely chopped**
- **15 graham crackers, each 2½-inches square**
- **½ cup semisweet chocolate chips**

Preheat oven to 375°F. Grease a 13 × 9 × 2-inch baking pan.

Stir flour, salt, and baking soda together in 1½-quart bowl. Beat butter, sugar, and eggs in large mixing bowl until light and fluffy. Stir in half of flour mixture. Mix in ⅓ cup milk and 1 teaspoon vanilla. Stir in remaining flour mixture. Pour half of batter into small bowl. Stir in ½ teaspoon vanilla, melted chocolate, almonds, and ⅓ cup milk.

Spread into prepared pan. Arrange graham crackers in one layer on top of chocolate mixture. Stir chocolate pieces into remaining batter. Drop by tablespoons onto graham crackers. Spread evenly to form a third layer. Bake for 20 minutes, or until lightly browned. Cool in pan before cutting into bars.

Easy Graham Bars

MAKES 30 BARS

- **3 cups fine graham cracker crumbs**
- **1 cup sugar**
- **1 cup milk**
- **1 cup (6 ounces) semisweet chocolate chips**
- **½ cup pecans or walnuts, chopped**
- **¼ cup butter or margarine, softened**
- **1 teaspoon vanilla**

Preheat oven to 350°F. Grease well a 13 × 9 × 2-inch baking pan.

Combine all ingredients. Mix well. Spread mixture in prepared pan. Bake 30 minutes, or until bar pulls from sides of pan. Cool. Cut into bars.

Chocolate Chewies

MAKES 4½ DOZEN COOKIES

- **2 tablespoons butter or margarine**
- **1 package (12 ounces) semisweet chocolate chips**
- **1 can (14 ounces) sweetened condensed milk**
- **1 cup all-purpose flour**
- **1½ teaspoons vanilla**

Preheat oven to 325° F. Heavily grease a cookie sheet.

In double boiler over medium heat, melt butter or margarine and chocolate chips. Remove from heat and add remaining ingredients, mixing well. Drop by teaspoonfuls onto cookie sheet. Bake for 10 to 12 minutes. Cool on wire rack. Store in airtight container.

Chocolate Macaroons

MAKES ABOUT 4 DOZEN COOKIES

- **3 ounces (3 squares) unsweetened baking chocolate**
- **3 eggs**
- **1½ cups sugar**
- **1 teaspoon vanilla**
- **⅛ teaspoon salt**
- **2 cups nuts, grated**

Preheat oven to 350°F. Cover cookie sheets with greased brown paper.

Melt chocolate in double boiler, over medium heat; let cool. Using mixer, beat eggs until well blended. Gradually add sugar and continue beating until light colored and thick, about 7 minutes. Mix in chocolate, vanilla, and salt. Fold in nuts.

Drop by half teaspoonfuls, 2 inches apart, onto prepared cookie sheets. Bake until firm to the touch, for 15 to 20 minutes.

Florentines

MAKES 3½ TO 4 DOZEN COOKIES

½ cup butter
¾ cup sugar
3 eggs
¾ teaspoon almond extract
1 teaspoon orange peel, grated
2½ cups all-purpose flour
1½ teaspoons baking powder
¼ teaspoon salt
1 cup ground almonds
1 cup semisweet chocolate chips
2 tablespoons hot water

Preheat oven to 375°F. Lightly grease cookie sheets.

Cream butter and sugar. Add eggs one at a time, beating well after each addition. Beat in almond extract and orange peel. Sift flour, baking powder, and salt together, and add to creamed mixture; stir well to combine. Add almonds and stir well. Refrigerate dough for several hours.

Form dough into loaves 1½ inches wide and ½ inch thick. Make sure loaves are several inches apart, as the cookies spread in baking. Make loaves as long as your cookie sheet allows, but leave at least an inch space between end of loaf and edge of cookie sheet to prevent burning. Bake 12 to 15 minutes, or until lightly browned and a toothpick inserted in center of loaf comes out clean. While still warm, cut loaves into ¾-inch strips and cool on a cake rack.

Melt chocolate chips over hot water, stirring occasionally. When completely melted, stir in just enough boiling water to make a thick mixture with consistency of layer-cake icing. Dip both ends of the cookie strips in chocolate and allow to dry on a rack until chocolate has hardened.

Chocolate Chip Cookies

MAKES ABOUT 4 DOZEN COOKIES

1½ cups all-purpose flour
½ teaspoon baking powder
¼ teaspoon salt
½ cup butter or margarine, softened
1 cup brown sugar, firmly packed
½ teaspoon vanilla
⅔ cup milk
½ package (6 ounces) semisweet chocolate chips
½ cup walnuts, chopped

Preheat oven to 350°F. Grease cookie sheets.

Stir flour, baking powder, and salt together. Set aside. Beat butter, sugar, and vanilla together until fluffy. Add flour mixture and milk. Stir until well blended. Mix in semisweet chocolate pieces and walnuts.

Drop by heaping teaspoonfuls onto greased cookie sheets. Flatten slightly, as the cookies do not spread in baking. Bake for 13 to 15 minutes, or until browned. Remove immediately to cooling racks. Cool thoroughly before storing in tightly covered container.

Florentines

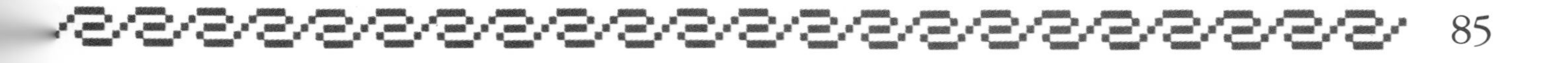

Rocky Road Squares ✓

MAKES ABOUT 40 SQUARES

- **⅔ cup milk**
- **1 cup sugar**
- **1 package (12 ounces) semisweet chocolate chips**
- **2 tablespoons butter or margarine**
- **2 cups dry roasted peanuts**
- **1 package (10½ ounces) miniature marshmallows**

Grease a 13 × 9 × 2-inch baking pan.

In 3-quart saucepan, combine milk and sugar. Cook over medium heat just to boiling. Remove from heat. Stir in chocolate chips and butter until melted. Mix in nuts. Empty marshmallows into buttered pan. Pour chocolate mixture over. Toss to coat marshmallows and nuts. Spread evenly. Chill until firm. Cut into squares. Cover and store in refrigerator.

Chocolate Nut Cookies

MAKES 3 DOZEN COOKIES

- **½ cup butter or margarine, softened**
- **½ cup brown sugar**
- **¼ cup honey**
- **1 teaspoon vanilla**
- **1 egg, beaten**
- **2 ounces (2 squares) unsweetened baking chocolate, melted**
- **¾ cup whole-wheat pastry flour**
- **2 tablespoons nonfat dry milk powder**
- **½ teaspoon salt**
- **⅛ teaspoon baking soda**
- **¾ cup peanuts (unsalted), chopped**
- **1 cup sunflower seeds (unsalted)**

Preheat oven to 375°F. Lightly grease cookie sheets.

Cream butter, sugar, and honey together. Blend in vanilla, egg, and chocolate. Stir flour, milk powder, salt, and soda together. Add to creamed mixture; mix well. Stir in peanuts and sunflower seeds.

Drop by teaspoonfuls onto prepared cookie sheets, about 2 inches apart. Bake 8 to 10 minutes. Remove from pan to cool.

Choco-oatmeal Cookies

MAKES 3½ DOZEN COOKIES

- **¾ cup butter or margarine, softened**
- **1½ cups brown sugar, firmly packed**
- **2 eggs**
- **1¾ cups all-purpose flour**
- **2 tablespoons cocoa**
- **1 tablespoon cinnamon**
- **¾ teaspoon baking soda**
- **¼ teaspoon salt**
- **1½ cups oatmeal**
- **1 cup (6 ounces) semisweet chocolate chips**

Preheat oven to 375°F. Lightly grease cookie sheets.

In medium bowl, sift flour, cocoa, cinnamon, baking soda, and salt together. Set aside. In large bowl, beat butter or margarine and brown sugar until light and fluffy. Beat in eggs, one at a time. Gradually add dry ingredients, blending well. Stir in oatmeal and chocolate chips.

Drop by rounded teaspoonfuls onto prepared cookie sheets. Bake 10 to 12 minutes, until golden brown. Cool 1 minute before removing from cookie sheet.

Old-fashioned Chocolate Chip Drop Cookies

MAKES 6½ TO 7 DOZEN COOKIES

- **1½ cups all-purpose flour, sifted**
- **½ teaspoon baking soda**
- **¼ teaspoon salt**
- **½ cup butter or margarine, softened**
- **1 cup brown sugar, firmly packed**
- **1 egg, well beaten**
- **½ teaspoon vanilla**
- **¼ cup milk**
- **1 cup (6 ounces) semisweet chocolate chips**
- **½ cup nuts, chopped**

Preheat oven to 375°F. Grease cookie sheets.

Sift flour with baking soda and salt. Set aside. In large bowl, beat butter or margarine and brown sugar until light and fluffy. Beat in egg and vanilla, mixing well. Add about ⅓ of flour mixture. Stir until smooth. Add ½ of milk. Repeat until all flour and milk are used. Fold in chocolate chips and nuts.

Drop by teaspoonfuls onto greased cookie sheets about 2 inches apart. Bake on middle oven rack for 9 to 11 minutes, or until light brown. Let stand 1 minute before removing from cookie sheet.

"Hearty" Chocolate Chip Cookies

MAKES ABOUT 5 DOZEN COOKIES

1½ cups all-purpose flour
1 teaspoon salt
½ teaspoon baking soda
1 cup butter or margarine, softened
¾ cup brown sugar, firmly packed
½ cup granulated sugar
2 eggs
1 teaspoon vanilla
2 cups natural cereal, any variety
1 package (12 ounces) semisweet chocolate chips
1 cup nuts, chopped

Preheat oven to 375°F. Grease cookie sheets.

In small bowl, stir flour, salt, and baking soda together. In large bowl, cream together butter or margarine, and sugars. Add eggs and vanilla, and beat until smooth. Mix in flour mixture, and blend well. Stir in cereal, chocolate chips, and nuts. Refrigerate batter about 1 hour or until chilled.

Drop chilled batter by teaspoonfuls onto greased cookie sheets. Bake for 10 minutes. Remove to cooling racks. Cool completely before storing.

Chocolate Chip Foursome

MAKES ABOUT 3 DOZEN COOKIES

½ cup brown sugar, firmly packed
½ cup sugar
½ cup butter or margarine
½ cup shortening
1 teaspoon vanilla
1 egg
1½ cups all-purpose flour
1 teaspoon baking soda
¼ teaspoon salt
1 cup semisweet chocolate chips
1 ounce (1 square) unsweetened baking chocolate, melted
½ cup pecans, chopped

Preheat oven to 375°F. In large bowl, cream sugars, butter, and shortening together until light and fluffy. Blend in egg and vanilla. Stir flour, baking soda, and salt together. Combine with sugar mixture, mixing well.

Divide dough into 2 parts; place in small bowls. Add chocolate chips to one, melted chocolate and pecans to the other. Refrigerate dough ½ hour. Shape dough into ½ teaspoon balls. Arrange 2 of each flavor together to form a four-leaf clover. Place on ungreased cookie sheet.

Bake for 8 to 10 minutes, until golden brown. Let cool 1 minute before removing from cookie sheets.

Chocolate Raisin Clusters

MAKES 3½ TO 4 DOZEN COOKIES

- **1½ cups light or dark raisins**
- **½ cup shortening**
- **1 cup brown sugar, firmly packed**
- **1 egg**
- **2 ounces (2 squares) unsweetened baking chocolate**
- **1¼ cups all-purpose flour, sifted**
- **½ teaspoon baking powder**
- **½ teaspoon salt**
- **⅓ cup milk**
- **1 teaspoon vanilla**
- **½ cup walnuts, chopped**

Preheat oven to 350°F. Grease cookie sheets.

Rinse and drain raisins. Cream shortening and sugar together. Add egg and beat thoroughly. Stir in melted chocolate. Sift flour with baking powder and salt. Blend into creamed mixture alternately with milk. Add vanilla, raisins and walnuts.

Drop by teaspoonfuls onto prepared cookie sheets. Bake about 15 minutes. Remove to wire rack to cool.

Chocolate Sour Cream Cookies

MAKES 5½ DOZEN COOKIES

- **3 ounces (3 squares) unsweetened baking chocolate**
- **½ cup milk**
- **¾ cup brown sugar, firmly packed**
- **½ cup butter or margarine, softened**
- **¾ cup dairy sour cream**
- **1½ teaspoons vanilla**
- **1 egg**
- **2 cups all-purpose flour**
- **½ teaspoon baking soda**
- **¼ teaspoon salt**

Frosting

- **1 ounce (1 square) unsweetened baking chocolate**
- **¼ cup dairy sour cream**
- **2 tablespoons margarine or butter**
- **1 to 2 tablespoons milk**
- **2 cups confectioners' sugar**
- **¾ teaspoon vanilla**

Preheat oven to 375°F. Grease and slightly flour cookie sheets.

In small saucepan, melt chocolate over low heat, stirring constantly. Remove from heat; cool. In large bowl, cream brown sugar and butter until light and fluffy; blend in sour cream, vanilla, egg, and melted chocolate. Blend flour, baking soda, and salt together; then add to creamed mixture. Drop dough by teaspoonfuls onto prepared cookie sheets. Bake 5 to 10 minutes, or until set. Cool.

To make frosting, combine chocolate, sour cream, butter, and milk in small saucepan. Stir constantly over low heat until melted. Remove from heat and stir in confectioners' sugar and vanilla.

Chocolate Sundae Cookies

MAKES 3 DOZEN COOKIES

- **2 ounces (2 squares) unsweetened baking chocolate**
- **1½ cups all-purpose flour, sifted**
- **¼ teaspoon salt**
- **½ teaspoon baking soda**
- **½ cup butter or margarine**
- **⅔ cup brown sugar, firmly packed**
- **1 egg**
- **¼ cup maraschino cherry juice**
- **2 tablespoons milk**
- **½ cup pecans, chopped**
- **¼ cup maraschino cherries, drained and chopped**
- **18 marshmallows, halved**
- **Chocolate Icing (see Index)**
- **3 dozen pecan halves**

Preheat oven to 350°F.

In double boiler, melt chocolate over medium heat; let cool. Sift flour, salt, and soda together; set aside. Cream butter. Gradually add sugar and continue creaming until light and fluffy. Beat in egg. Blend in dry ingredients alternately with cherry juice and milk, beginning and ending with dry ingredients. Stir in chocolate, chopped pecans, and cherries.

Drop by rounded teaspoonfuls, 2 inches apart, onto ungreased cookie sheets. Bake 12 to 15 minutes, or until set. Place marshmallow half, cut side down, on hot cookie. Let cool. Ice with Chocolate Frosting. Top each cookie with pecan half.

Double Chocolate Cookies

MAKES ABOUT 3½ DOZEN COOKIES

- **½ cup brown sugar, firmly packed**
- **½ cup sugar**
- **¾ cup margarine or butter, softened**
- **1½ teaspoons vanilla**
- **1 egg**
- **1¾ cups all-purpose flour**
- **¼ cup cocoa**
- **1 teaspoon baking soda**
- **¼ teaspoon salt**
- **6 ounces (1 cup) semisweet chocolate chips**
- **½ cup pecans, chopped**

Preheat oven to 375°F.

Cream sugars and margarine or butter in large bowl until light and fluffy. Beat in vanilla and egg. In medium bowl, combine flour, cocoa, baking soda, and salt; blend well. Add dry ingredients to creamed mixture gradually, beating well after each addition. Stir in chocolate chips and nuts.

Place teaspoonfuls onto ungreased cookie sheets. Bake 8 to 10 minutes, or until set. Let stand 1 minute before removing from cookie sheets.

Chocolate and Vanilla Refrigerator Cookies

MAKES 40 COOKIES

- **1 cup butter, softened**
- **1 cup sugar**
- **3 eggs**
- **4 cups all-purpose flour, sifted**
- **½ teaspoon salt**
- **1 teaspoon soda**
- **1 teaspoon baking powder**
- **1 teaspoon vanilla**
- **1 ounce (1 square) unsweetened baking chocolate, melted**

Preheat oven to 400°F. Lightly flour a cookie sheet.

Combine butter and sugar in large bowl and beat with electric mixer until creamy. Add eggs, one at a time, beating after each addition until thoroughly blended. Sift flour, salt, soda, and baking powder together, then add to creamed mixture gradually, mixing well.

Divide dough in half. Add vanilla to one portion and blend thoroughly. Add chocolate to remaining portion and mix well.

Shape each portion into 2 rolls, 1 inch in diameter. Place a vanilla and a chocolate roll side by side; then place a vanilla roll on top of the chocolate one, and a chocolate roll on top of the first vanilla one. Press all 4 rolls together and wrap in waxed paper. Chill in refrigerator overnight.

Cut in ¼-inch slices and place on prepared cookie sheet. Bake 10 to 12 minutes, or until vanilla portion is slightly browned. Remove from baking sheet immediately and cool on a rack.

Fudge Brownie Cookies

MAKES 5 DOZEN COOKIES

- **1 package (12 ounces) semisweet chocolate chips**
- **2 tablespoons butter or margarine**
- **1 can (14 ounces) sweetened condensed milk**
- **1 cup all-purpose flour**
- **1 teaspoon vanilla**
- **1 cup walnuts, chopped**

Preheat oven to 325°F. Grease cookie sheets well.

In a medium saucepan over low heat, melt chocolate chips and butter or margarine. Remove from heat and add sweetened condensed milk, flour, and vanilla. Stir in nuts.

Drop by teaspoonfuls on prepared cookie sheets. Bake 8 to 10 minutes. Cool 1 minute before removing from cookie sheets. Store in airtight container.

Old-fashioned Drop Cookies

MAKES 5 DOZEN COOKIES

- **2 cups all-purpose flour**
- **1½ cups brown sugar, firmly packed**
- **1 teaspoon salt**
- **½ teaspoon baking soda**
- **1 cup butter or margarine, softened**
- **2 eggs**
- **1 teaspoon vanilla**
- **3 cups natural cereal, plain, coconut or raisin**
- **1 cup (6 ounces) semisweet chocolate chips**

Preheat oven to 375°F. Grease cookie sheets.

Stir flour, brown sugar, salt, and baking soda together. Mix in butter, eggs, and vanilla until smooth. Stir in cereal and chocolate chips. Drop by teaspoonfuls, about 2 inches apart, onto prepared cookie sheet. Bake 10 to 12 minutes.

Variation: Cookie batter may be poured into 13 × 9-inch baking pan and baked at 350°F 25 to 30 minutes, or until knife inserted 3 inches from edge comes out clean.

Chocolate Meringue Squares ✓

MAKES 20 TO 25 SQUARES

Chocolate Batter

- **7 tablespoons margarine or butter**
- **⅓ cup sugar**
- **3 egg yolks**
- **⅔ cup flour**
- **3 tablespoons cocoa**
- **2 teaspoons baking powder**
- **¼ cup milk**

Meringue Batter

- **3 egg whites**
- **⅓ cup sugar**
- **½ cup hazelnuts, chopped**

Preheat oven to 350° F. Cover a baking pan with baking paper. Grease it with margarine.

Beat margarine and sugar together until airy. Add egg yolks, one at a time.

Mix flour, cocoa, and baking powder together. Alternate adding this mixture and the milk to the egg-yolk mixture. Spread the batter into the baking pan, using a rubber spatula.

Whip egg whites into dry peaks. Whip in sugar. Spread meringue batter over the chocolate batter. Sprinkle with nuts. Bake in the center of oven for 25 to 30 minutes. Let cake cool. Cut it into squares with a sharp knife.

Chocolate Meringue Squares

Ice Creams

Chocolate Ice Cream

MAKES 2 QUARTS

3 tall cans (12 fluid ounces each) evaporated milk, divided usage
2½ ounces (2½ squares) unsweetened baking chocolate
2 eggs
1 cup sugar
1 tablespoon vanilla

Combine 1 can evaporated milk and chocolate in small saucepan. Cook over medium heat, stirring frequently, until chocolate melts and mixture is smooth.

Meanwhile, beat eggs and sugar in large mixing bowl until blended. Stir in hot chocolate mixture. Stir in remaining cans evaporated milk and vanilla. Refrigerate until well chilled.

Pour into ice cream freezer container. Churn and freeze according to manufacturer's directions.

NOTE: The ice cream recipes in the book were tested using an electric-powered ice cream freezer. A mechanical hand-crank freezer may be used. The mixtures are CHURN-FROZEN, which usually produces a much smoother finished product. Refer to your manufacturer's directions for additional information about freezing ice cream.

Chocolate Chip Ice Cream Sandwiches

MAKES 12 ICE CREAM SANDWICHES

- **½ cup brown sugar, firmly packed**
- **¼ cup sugar**
- **¾ cup margarine or butter, softened**
- **½ teaspoon vanilla**
- **1 egg**
- **1¾ cups all-purpose flour**
- **¼ cup cocoa**
- **1 teaspoon baking soda**
- **¼ teaspoon salt**
- **6 ounces (1 cup) semisweet chocolate chips**
- **½ cup nuts, chopped**
- **1 quart vanilla ice cream, softened**

Preheat oven to 375° F. Cream sugars and margarine or butter in large bowl until light and fluffy. Beat in vanilla and egg. Combine flour, cocoa, baking soda, and salt; blend well. Add dry ingredients to creamed mixture. Stir in chocolate chips and nuts.

Drop by tablespoonfuls onto ungreased cookie sheets. Bake for 8 to 10 minutes, or until set. Let stand 1 minute before removing from cookie sheets. Cool completely. Place 1 scoop ice cream between 2 cookies. Wrap individually in plastic wrap and freeze 1 hour, until firm.

Cinnamon Chocolate Ice Cream I

MAKES ABOUT 2 QUARTS

- **3 tall cans (12 fluid ounces each) evaporated milk, divided usage**
- **2½ ounces (2½ squares) unsweetened baking chocolate**
- **2 eggs**
- **1 cup sugar**
- **½ teaspoon cinnamon**
- **¼ teaspoon nutmeg**

In small saucepan, combine one can of evaporated milk and chocolate. Cook over medium heat, stirring frequently, until chocolate melts and mixture is smooth.

Meanwhile, in large mixing bowl, beat eggs, sugar, cinnamon, and nutmeg together. Stir in hot chocolate mixture. Add remaining 2 cups of evaporated milk and mix well. Refrigerate mixture until well chilled.

Pour into ice cream freezer container. Churn and freeze according to manufacturer's directions.

Cinnamon Chocolate Ice Cream II

MAKES 2 QUARTS

4½ cups heavy cream, divided usage
2½ ounces (2½ squares) unsweetened baking chocolate
2 eggs
1 cup sugar
½ teaspoon ground cinnamon
¼ teaspoon ground nutmeg

In small saucepan, combine 1½ cups cream and chocolate. Cook over medium heat, stirring frequently, until chocolate melts and mixture is smooth.

Meanwhile, beat eggs, sugar, cinnamon, and nutmeg in large mixing bowl until well blended. Stir in hot chocolate mixture. Stir in remaining cream. Refrigerate until well chilled. Pour into ice cream freezer container. Churn and freeze according to manufacturer's directions.

Chocolate Sundae

MAKES 1 SERVING

1 scoop chocolate ice cream
2 tablespoons chocolate fudge sauce
1 tablespoon whipped topping
1 teaspoon pecans, chopped
1 maraschino cherry

Place one scoop ice cream into a dessert dish. Drizzle with chocolate sauce. Top with whipped topping, pecans, and a cherry.

Royal Dessert

MAKES 4 SERVINGS

8 medium meringues (see below)
8 balls vanilla ice cream
¾ cup chocolate sauce
¾ cup whipped cream
Grated semisweet baking chocolate

Alternate the meringues and ice cream in a tall glass. Pour chocolate sauce over them. Top with a dab of whipped cream and the grated cooking chocolate. Serve with bananas or fresh berries, if desired.

To make meringues: Beat 2 egg whites with electric mixer until soft peaks form. Gradually add ¼ cup sugar, beating until stiff peaks form. Place meringues on a cookie sheet lined with baking paper. Bake at 300° F for 30 to 35 minutes.

Royal Dessert

Mint Chip Ice Cream

MAKES ABOUT 2 QUARTS

- **3 eggs**
- **1½ cups sugar**
- **2 tall cans (12 fluid ounces each) evaporated milk**
- **¾ teaspoon peppermint extract**
- **⅛ teaspoon green food coloring**
- **1½ cups (6 ounces) milk chocolate, grated**

In large mixing bowl, beat eggs and sugar together. Stir in evaporated milk, extract, and food coloring. Gently stir in grated chocolate until just mixed. Refrigerate mixture until well chilled.

Pour into ice cream freezer container. Churn and freeze according to manufacturer's directions.

German Chocolate Ice Cream

MAKES 2 QUARTS

- **2 ounces (2 squares) unsweetened baking chocolate**
- **¾ cup caramel topping**
- **2 eggs**
- **¼ cup sugar**
- **2 tall cans (12 fluid ounces each) evaporated milk, divided usage**
- **½ cup coconut, shredded**
- **1 cup pecans, chopped**

In small saucepan, melt chocolate. Add caramel and stir until smooth and creamy. Allow to cool.

Meanwhile, beat eggs and sugar in large mixing bowl. Add 1 can evaporated milk and beat until well blended. Slowly stir in cooled chocolate mixture. Add remaining can of evaporated milk. Refrigerate until well chilled.

Pour into ice cream freezer container. Churn and freeze according to manufacturer's directions. When ice cream is finished churning, stir in coconut and pecans.

Mocha Chocolate Ice Cream

MAKES 2 QUARTS

- **3 cups (24 ounces) heavy cream, divided usage**
- **2 ounces (2 squares) unsweetened baking chocolate**
- **2 to 3 tablespoons instant coffee granules**
- **2 eggs**
- **1 cup sugar**
- **1 cup pecans or almonds, chopped**

In small saucepan, combine 1 cup cream, chocolate, and coffee granules. Cook over medium heat, stirring frequently, until chocolate melts and mixture is smooth.

Meanwhile, beat eggs and sugar in large mixing bowl until well blended. Stir in hot chocolate mixture. Stir in remaining cream. Refrigerate until well chilled. Pour into ice cream freezer container. Churn and freeze according to manufacturer's directions. When ice cream is finished, stir in pecans.

Peanut Butter Chocolate Ice Cream

MAKES 2 QUARTS

3 cups (24 ounces) heavy cream, divided usage
2 ounces (2 squares) unsweetened baking chocolate
2 eggs
¾ cup sugar
4 to 6 tablespoons chunky peanut butter

In small saucepan, combine 1 cup cream and chocolate. Cook over medium heat, stirring frequently, until chocolate melts and mixture is smooth.

Meanwhile, beat eggs and sugar in large mixing bowl until well blended. Beat in peanut butter until smooth. Stir in hot chocolate mixture. Stir in remaining cream. Refrigerate until well chilled. Pour into ice cream freezer container. Churn and freeze according to manufacturer's direction.

Banana Split

MAKES 4 SERVINGS

4 bananas, halved lengthwise
½ pint chocolate ice cream
½ pint vanilla ice cream
½ pint strawberry ice cream
½ cup chocolate fudge sauce
½ cup strawberry topping
½ cup pineapple topping
¼ cup whipped topping
4 teaspoons nuts, chopped
4 maraschino cherries

Place 2 banana halves in 4 separate dessert dishes.

Place one scoop of each flavor ice cream over the bananas. Drizzle 2 tablespoons each topping onto desired ice creams. Top with 1 tablespoon whipped topping, 1 teaspoon nuts, and maraschino cherry on each.

Sundae Supreme

MAKES 4 SERVINGS

4 frozen waffles, any variety
Vanilla ice cream
Hot Fudge Sauce (see Index)
whipped topping, thawed
½ cup nuts, chopped
4 maraschino cherries

Toast waffles. Top each waffle with ice cream, Hot Fudge Sauce, whipped topping, chopped nuts, and 1 cherry.

Chocolate Milk Shake

MAKES 1 SERVING

1 cup milk
2 tablespoons chocolate syrup or chocolate malted milk powder
2 scoops (½ cup) chocolate ice cream
2 tablespoons whipped topping
Maraschino cherries
Chopped nuts (optional)

In blender, combine milk, chocolate syrup or malt, and ice cream. Mix on HIGH for 20 to 30 seconds, until well blended. Pour into tall glass. Top with whipped topping, maraschino cherry, and nuts if desired.

Sundae Supreme

Fondues and Dipped Fruit

Chocolate-covered Cherries

MAKES 4 DOZEN CHERRIES

- **3 tablespoons butter**
- **¼ cup milk**
- **1 teaspoon vanilla**
- **¼ teaspoon salt**
- **3 to 4 cups confectioners' sugar, sifted**
- **48 maraschino cherries, drained**
- **½ package (6 ounces) semisweet chocolate chips**

Melt butter over low heat. Stir in milk, vanilla, and salt. Remove from heat and gradually stir in sugar. Turn out onto a board, lightly sprinkled with confectioners' sugar; work with hands until smooth. Cover cherries completely by shaping about 2 teaspoons fondant around each cherry.

Melt semisweet chocolate in double boiler. Drop fondant-covered cherries into melted chocolate to cover. Remove from chocolate with two forks. Place on waxed paper to cool.

Note: To give chocolate a shiny, hard coating, add 1 to 2 tablespoons melted paraffin wax to chocolate.

Chocolate-covered Strawberries

MAKES 20 TO 24 STRAWBERRIES

- **3 tablespoons butter**
- **¼ cup milk**
- **1 teaspoon vanilla**
- **¼ teaspoon salt**
- **3 to 4 cups confectioners' sugar, sifted**
- **20 to 24 strawberries with green stems, completely dry**
- **½ package (6 ounces) semisweet chocolate chips**
- **2 tablespoons (1 ounce) paraffin wax**

Melt butter over low heat. Stir in milk, vanilla, and salt. Remove from heat and gradually stir in sugar until mixture is firm and holds its shape. Turn onto a board lightly sprinkled with powdered sugar. Work with hands until smooth. Shape about 2 teaspoons of fondant around each strawberry. Fondant should be at room temperature prior to dipping strawberries.

Melt semisweet chocolate chips and paraffin wax in double boiler. Dip fondant-covered strawberries into melted chocolate, leaving stem exposed. Place on waxed paper. Let cool. Carefully remove strawberries from waxed paper. Store in airtight container in refrigerator. Best if eaten within 2 to 3 days after preparing.

Chocolate-dipped Strawberries

MAKES 40 STRAWBERRIES

- **40 large fresh strawberries**
- **6 ounces semisweet chocolate, broken into coarse pieces**
- **1½ tablespoons vegetable oil (a tasteless variety)**

Rinse strawberries quickly and dry thoroughly. Spread them in a single layer on a dish towel, turning occasionally until they are completely free of moisture.

Do not remove hull. Have cookie sheet lined with waxed paper or wire cake racks ready to receive dipped berries.

Fill bottom of double boiler with several inches of water, until it comes up to the bottom of inserted pan or bowl. Bring water to boil before you insert the top pan. Remove from heat and insert top pot, with the chocolate and vegetable oil in it. Stir with rubber spatula until chocolate is thoroughly melted and satiny.

Holding the berry by its stem, dip it two-thirds of the way into chocolate, turning it so that you can still see some of the red at the top of the berry. Place it on its side on the waxed paper, or stand stem down on wire rack. If the chocolate drips too freely and does not adhere to berry, stir to cool further. The temperature should be between 86° and 90° F.

Ideally, your kitchen should not be too warm. It is helpful to place the pan or racks of berries in the refrigerator for 15 to 20 minutes to help set the chocolate. Try to dip the berries the afternoon you plan to use them. They do not keep well overnight.

Chocolate Fondue I

MAKES 6 TO 8 SERVINGS

- **12 ounces chocolate**
- **¾ cup cream**
- **1 to 2 tablespoons brandy or kirsch, *or* 2 teaspoons instant coffee**

Dippers

- **Pieces of cake (pound or angel food)**
- **Sliced bananas**
- **Pineapple chunks**
- **Marshmallows**
- **Mandarin orange segments**
- **Apple wedges**

In heavy saucepan, melt chocolate and cream over low heat, stirring until smooth. Remove from heat; stir in flavoring. Pour into fondue pot and use the above dippers.

Chocolate Fondue II

MAKES 6 TO 8 SERVINGS

- **2 bars (8 ounces each) milk chocolate**
- **⅔ cup milk**
- **⅛ teaspoon salt**
- **3 tablespoons crème de cacao or orange-flavored liqueur**

Dippers

- **Angel cake**
- **Pound cake**
- **Maraschino cherries**
- **Apples**
- **Marshmallows**
- **Bananas**
- **Strawberries**

Melt chocolate in medium saucepan over low heat. Add milk and salt. Cook until thickened, about 5 minutes. Stir constantly. Stir in liqueur. Pour into fondue pot and light burner. Serve with dippers.

Fondue Chips

MAKES 4 TO 6 SERVINGS

- **6 dessert crêpes**
- **Confectioners' sugar**
- **Chocolate Fondue**

Preheat oven to 400° F.

Cut each crêpe into 12 or 16 pieces. Place on a cookie sheet and bake 6 to 8 minutes, or until crisp. Remove from oven and sprinkle with sugar. Use with Chocolate Fondue.

Chocolate Fondue and Assorted Dippers

Pears in Chocolate Sauce

MAKES 6 SERVINGS

1 large can (29 ounces) pear halves

Chocolate Sauce
8 ounces (8 squares) semisweet chocolate
2 tablespoons hot water
1 tablespoon butter
1 egg yolk
½ cup heavy cream
1 egg white

Drain pear halves; arrange in 6 individual serving dishes.

Place chocolate in top of double boiler. Stir in hot water; melt chocolate over boiling water. Remove from heat. Stir in butter until melted. Add egg yolk and heavy cream. Beat egg white until stiff peaks form; fold into Chocolate Sauce.

Spoon Chocolate Sauce over pears. Serve immediately.

Chocolate-covered Pear Layer

MAKES 12 SERVINGS

10 canned pear halves, drained
1 9-inch yellow-cake layer
½ cup corn syrup
¼ cup hot water
¼ cup butter
1 (12-ounce) package chocolate chips
1 container (10 ounces) whipped topping

Slice each pear half into 3 equal slices. Arrange sliced pears in a circle around outer edge of cake layer.

Combine corn syrup, hot water, and butter in saucepan. Heat to boiling. Remove from heat; stir in chocolate chips until well blended. Cool to warm. Cover cake with warm glaze. Let glaze set before decorating with whipped topping.

Chocolate Mousse I

MAKES 8 SERVINGS

4 eggs, separated
½ cup sugar
¼ cup frozen concentrated orange juice
6 ounces plain dark chocolate
3 tablespoons strong black coffee
¾ cup unsalted butter, softened
Pinch of salt
1 tablespoon sugar
whipped topping

Beat egg yolks and sugar together until thick and pale. Beat in orange juice. Place bowl over very hot but not boiling water and stir or beat, clearing sides of bowl, until mixture thickens evenly and is too hot to touch. Remove from heat, place on ice or over cold water, and beat until cooled and like thick mayonnaise.

Melt chocolate over hot water. Remove from heat, and beat in butter gradually, making a smooth cream. Stir chocolate lightly into egg and sugar.

Beat egg whites until firm. Sprinkle on salt and a tablespoon sugar; beat again until stiff. Stir 1 tablespoon egg-white mixture into chocolate mixture. Then fold in the remainder. Turn into a prepared soufflé dish and allow to set. Decorate with whipped topping before serving.

Chocolate Mousse II

MAKES 8 SERVINGS

1 cup (6 ounces) semisweet chocolate chips
5 tablespoons boiling water
4 eggs, separated
2 tablespoons dark rum

Put chocolate pieces in blender. Mix on high speed for 6 seconds. Scrape sides; add boiling water; blend on high speed for 10 seconds. Add egg yolks and dark rum; blend 3 seconds, or until smooth.

Fold chocolate mixture into stiffly beaten egg whites. Spoon and chill 1 hour.

Chocolate Bavarois or Bavarian Cream

MAKES 6 SERVINGS

4 ounces (4 squares) unsweetened baking chocolate
1¼ cups milk
3 egg yolks *or* 1 whole egg and 1 yolk
¼ to ⅜ cup sugar
1½ tablespoons gelatin
4 tablespoons water
1 teaspoon vanilla *or* coffee flavoring
1¼ cups heavy cream

Grate chocolate and dissolve it in milk. Beat eggs and sugar until liquid, and make a thick-pouring custard with the flavored milk, straining back into the pan to cook and thicken. Do not allow to boil, or the eggs may curdle. Allow to cool.

Soak gelatin in the water for 5 minutes, then heat to dissolve. Stir the vanilla or coffee flavoring gently into cooled custard. Add the dissolved gelatin, stirring again as it cools.

Whip cream and fold lightly into custard mixture just before setting. Pour into a prepared mold or into glass dishes. Allow to set 1 to 2 hours.

Frozen Chocolate Soufflé

MAKES 4 SERVINGS

1 teaspoon vanilla
⅓ cup confectioners' sugar
3 egg yolks
3 to 4 ounces (3 to 4 squares) unsweetened baking chocolate
2 teaspoons instant coffee
¼ cup cocoa liqueur
1¼ cups whipping cream

Combine vanilla, sugar and egg yolks.

Place pan over simmering water. Beat vigorously until mixture becomes creamy but is still light and fluffy. Remove pan from double boiler. Beat until mixture is completely cold.

Melt the chocolate. Add it to egg mixture, together with instant coffee and liqueur. Chill mixture thoroughly. Beat cream until stiff. Stir chocolate mixture and cream together.

Tape pieces of heavy paper onto a 4-cup mold or individual soufflé dishes so that they stick up an inch over the edges. Fill the dishes with chocolate mixture to top of the paper edges. Place in freezer, but do not allow dessert to freeze completely. The inner part should still be unfrozen, which gives the dessert the character of a soufflé. It takes about 3 to 4 hours for small dishes, and longer if you use the larger mold.

Just before serving, remove paper edging. Decorate with small rolls of chocolate, or sift a little cocoa on top.

Frozen Chocolate Soufflé

Frozen Chocolate Mousse with Orange Cream

MAKES 8 SERVINGS

Chocolate Mousse
- **8 ounces (8 squares) semisweet chocolate**
- **6 egg yolks**
- **6 egg whites**

Orange Cream
- **10 ounces whipped topping**
- **1 can (6 ounces) frozen orange juice**
- **1 package ladyfingers**

Prepare mousse first. Slowly melt semisweet chocolate over low heat or over a double boiler. Stir egg yolks, one at a time, into the warm, liquidy chocolate. Let mixture totally cool before folding in egg whites, which have been beaten into stiff peaks.

Fold thawed orange juice into whipped topping.

Place ladyfingers standing up, tightly together, around a round, high 8-cup mold. Alternate spooning in chocolate mousse and orange cream in layers. Start with chocolate mousse. Place pan in freezer for at least 12 hours.

Turn out mousse upside down onto a plate. Decorate with orange slices or wedges, which can be dipped into melted chocolate for added effect.

Icings and Frostings

Chocolate Cream Cheese Frosting

very good

MAKES ENOUGH FOR TWO 8- OR 9-INCH CAKES

- **1 package (8 ounces) cream cheese, softened**
- **¼ cup milk**
- **1 teaspoon vanilla**
- **2 cups confectioners' sugar**
- **1 cup (6 ounces) chocolate chips, melted**
- **1 container (10 ounces) whipped topping**

In medium bowl, beat cream cheese and milk until light and creamy. Add vanilla. Gradually add confectioners' sugar, mixing well. Stir in chocolate. Fold in whipped topping. Keep refrigerated.

Fudge Frosting

MAKES ENOUGH FOR TWO 8- OR 9-INCH CAKES

- **2 ounces (2 squares) unsweetened cooking chocolate**
- **1 cup milk**
- **2 cups sugar**
- **⅛ teaspoon salt**
- **2 tablespoons white corn syrup**
- **2 tablespoons butter**
- **1 teaspoon vanilla**

Add chocolate to milk. Cook slowly until smooth and blended, stirring constantly. Add sugar, salt, and corn syrup. Stir until sugar is dissolved and mixture boils. Continue cooking until mixture forms a very soft ball when a little is dropped in cold water. Add butter and vanilla. Cool to lukewarm. Beat until thick enough to spread.

Chocolate Icing

MAKES ENOUGH FOR TOPS AND SIDES OF TWO, 9-INCH LAYERS

- **½ cup margarine**
- **1 pound confectioners' sugar, sifted**
- **4 tablespoons milk**
- **1 ounce premelted chocolate**

Cream margarine until smooth. Beat in confectioners' sugar, ½ cup at a time, beating well after each addition. Beat in milk and chocolate until icing becomes light and fluffy.

Quick Fudge Frosting

MAKES ENOUGH FOR 8-INCH SQUARE CAKE

- **1 package (6 ounces) semisweet chocolate pieces**
- **⅔ cup (½ of 15-ounce can) sweetened condensed milk**
- **1 tablespoon water**

Heat ingredients in top of double boiler. Stir until chocolate is melted and mixture is smooth. Remove from heat; cool in pan of ice and water.

Chocolate Fudge Frosting

MAKES ENOUGH FOR 9-INCH SQUARE CAKE

- **6 tablespoons milk**
- **1 tablespoon butter**
- **2½ cups confectioners' sugar**
- **½ cup cocoa**
- **⅛ teaspoon salt**
- **¾ teaspoon vanilla**

In saucepan over low heat, combine milk and butter until butter melts. Meanwhile, combine sugar, cocoa, and salt. Remove saucepan from heat. Stir in the sugar mixture, about ¼ cup at a time. Stir in vanilla. Beat until smooth and creamy.

Sour Cream Chocolate Frosting

MAKES ENOUGH FOR TWO 8- OR 9-INCH CAKES

- **2 packages (12 ounces) semisweet chocolate pieces**
- **1 cup thick sour cream**
- **1 teaspoon vanilla**
- **¼ teaspoon almond extract**
- **⅛ teaspoon salt**

Melt chocolate pieces and cool slightly. Blend chocolate into sour cream. Add vanilla, almond extract, and salt; blend well.

Chocolate Icing

Sauces

Basic Chocolate Sauce

MAKES 2 CUPS

- **¼ cup brown sugar, firmly packed**
- **2 cups chocolate chips**
- **¼ cup water**
- **½ cup butter**
- **2 teaspoons vanilla**

Combine brown sugar, chocolate, and water in top of double boiler over boiling water and stir until smooth. Cut butter into small pieces and beat it into chocolate mixture. Stir in vanilla. Cover tightly and let stand over warm water until ready to serve. Cool and use, as frosting, if desired.

Chocolate Marshmallow Sauce

MAKES 1½ CUPS

- **2 cups miniature marshmallows**
- **1 cup (6 ounces) semisweet chocolate chips**
- **¼ cup sugar**
- **⅔ cup milk**
- **2 tablespoons butter**
- **1 teaspoon vanilla**
- **Dash salt**

In heavy saucepan or double boiler, combine all ingredients. Cook over medium heat, stirring constantly until marshmallows have melted. Continue to cook until thickened. Serve warm over ice cream.

Note: Twenty large marshmallows may be used in place of the miniature marshmallows.

Chocolate Sauce with Honey

MAKES ABOUT 1 CUP

- **4 ounces (4 squares) unsweetened baking chocolate**
- **1 tablespoon Cointreau**
- **Pinch of salt**
- **¾ cup strained honey**
- **⅓ cup chopped almonds, toasted**

Combine chocolate and Cointreau in top of a double boiler and cook over hot water until chocolate melts. Add salt and honey and cook, stirring constantly, until smooth. Stir in almonds, then cover. Remove from heat and allow to stand for 20 minutes.

Serve warm over plain sponge cake, vanilla ice cream, or cream-filled choux pastries.

Chocolate Sauce De Luxe

MAKES 4 CUPS

- **½ cup butter**
- **3 ounces (3 squares) unsweetened baking chocolate**
- **1 pound confectioners' sugar**
- **⅛ teaspoon salt**
- **1 can (14½ ounces) evaporated milk, undiluted**
- **1½ teaspoons vanilla**

Melt butter and chocolate together in double boiler over medium heat. Add sugar, salt, and evaporated milk alternately, mixing thoroughly. Cook for 30 to 35 minutes at 175°F, stirring occasionally. Stir in vanilla.

This chocolate sauce will keep several weeks, covered, in refrigerator. Bring to room temperature before serving.

Chocolate Mint Sauce

MAKES 2 CUPS

- **2 cups sugar**
- **Dash of salt**
- **2 ounces (2 squares) unsweetened baking chocolate**
- **¾ cup milk**
- **1 tablespoon butter**
- **¼ cup peppermint candy, crushed**

Combine sugar, salt, chocolate, milk, and butter. Heat slowly, stirring until sugar is dissolved and chocolate melted. Boil, covered, 2 minutes; then boil, uncovered, until a small amount forms a very soft ball when dropped into cold water (230°F). Remove from heat.

Add crushed mints and beat slightly. Serve hot or warm. If sauce seems too thick, dilute with a small amount of cream.

Chocolate Rum Sauce

MAKES 2½ CUPS

2 cups sugar
¼ cup cocoa
Pinch of salt
1 tablespoon white corn syrup
½ cup milk
1 tablespoon butter
6 tablespoons rum

Combine sugar, cocoa, and salt in heavy saucepan and mix well. Stir in corn syrup and milk until well blended. Place over medium heat and bring to a slow boil, stirring constantly. Boil for about 2 minutes, or until all sugar is melted.

Remove from heat and stir in butter. Add rum slowly, stirring until well blended. Serve hot or cold.

Hot Fudge Sauce I

MAKES ABOUT 1½ CUPS

1 cup heavy whipping cream
6 tablespoons lightly salted butter, cut into small pieces
½ cup brown sugar
3 ounces sugar
1 cup cocoa, sifted
½ teaspoon vanilla

Mix all ingredients together in a saucepan. Heat over medium heat, stirring until butter is melted and mixture is smooth. Raise heat, and bring just to a boil. Reduce heat and stir with a whisk continuously over low heat for 8 minutes. Serve hot.

Store in glass or plastic in refrigerator. Reheat to use.

Hot Fudge Sauce II

MAKES 1⅔ CUPS

1 cup (6 ounces) semisweet chocolate chips
¾ cup milk
¼ cup sugar
¼ cup butter or margarine

In heavy saucepan, combine all ingredients. Stir over low heat until chocolate is completely melted. Serve warm.

Hot Fudge Sauce

Beverages

Chocolate Soda

MAKES 4 SERVINGS

- **1 bottle (32 ounces) lemon-lime soda, chilled**
- **½ cup chocolate syrup**
- **1 pint chocolate ice cream**
- **¼ cup whipped topping**
- **4 maraschino cherries**

In 4 tall glasses, combine ½ cup lemon-lime soda and 2 tablespoons chocolate syrup. Add 2 scoops chocolate ice cream; fill glasses with remaining soda. Top with 1 tablespoon whipped topping and maraschino cherry.

Chocolate Ice Cream Soda

MAKES 1 SODA

- **3 tablespoons chocolate syrup**
- **1 tablespoon cream**
- **2 tablespoons vanilla ice cream**
- **Soda water**

Mix syrup and cream in tall glass. Add ice cream. Add soda water. Stir well.

Hot Chocolate Mexican-style

MAKES 4 SERVINGS

2 ounces (2 squares) unsweetened baking chocolate
½ teaspoon vanilla
1 teaspoon ground cinnamon
4 tablespoons heavy cream
2 cups milk
2 egg yolks
2 tablespoons sugar
3 ounces brandy
4 cinnamon sticks

In saucepan, combine chocolate, vanilla, cinnamon, and cream; place over very low heat, stirring until chocolate is melted. Add milk slowly to chocolate mixture; mix well. Warm over very low heat. Do not allow mixture to boil.

Beat egg yolks and sugar until foamy. Slowly pour part of chocolate mixture into egg yolks, beating well. Pour egg-yolk mixture back into saucepan; beat. Add brandy to chocolate mixture; beat until mixture is frothy. Serve hot chocolate immediately in small cups with cinnamon sticks used as stirrers.

Little Chocolate Pots

MAKES 6 SERVINGS

1½ cups milk
2 cups chocolate chips
2 eggs
¼ cup sugar
Pinch of salt

Pour milk in heavy saucepan and heat to boiling point. Combine remaining ingredients in blender container. Pour in the hot milk, then blend at low speed for 1 minute or until smooth. Pour into 6 custard cups, then chill for at least 2 hours before serving.

Chocolate Brandy

MAKES ABOUT 1½ CUPS

2 scoops chocolate ice cream
1 cup plain yogurt
2 tablespoons brandy
whipped topping
Cocoa

Place ice cream, yogurt, and brandy in blender; blend until smooth. Pour into tall glass. Garnish with whipped topping and a pinch of cocoa.

Cafe Royal

MAKES 5 SERVINGS

4 cups water
½ cup (3 ounces) semisweet chocolate chips
½ cup sugar
½ teaspoon ground cinnamon
¼ teaspoon ground nutmeg
1 tablespoon instant coffee granules
1 cup milk
½ teaspoon vanilla
¼ cup Kahlua or other coffee-flavored liqueur, optional
whipped topping, thawed
Ground cinnamon

In heavy saucepan, combine water, chocolate chips, sugar, cinnamon, and nutmeg. Bring mixture to a boil over medium heat, stirring frequently. Continue to boil until chocolate is completely melted. Add coffee granules, stirring until dissolved.

Reduce heat and gradually stir in milk. Stir in vanilla and liqueur, if desired. Pour into mugs; top with whipped topping and sprinkle with cinnamon.

Chocolate Mocha Drink

MAKES 4 SERVINGS

⅓ cup water
¼ cup sugar
2 tablespoons unsweetened cocoa powder
½ cup milk
2 tablespoons semisweet chocolate chips
Hot coffee
whipped topping, thawed
Semisweet chocolate chips

In saucepan, combine water, sugar, and cocoa. Simmer mixture over medium heat 2 minutes, stirring frequently. Reduce heat and add milk in a slow stream, beating vigorously, until well combined. Add 2 tablespoons chocolate chips. Continue to heat until chocolate is completely melted, but do not boil.

Divide mixture among 4 heatproof glasses and then fill with hot coffee. Garnish each drink with a dollop of whipped topping, and sprinkle with chocolate chips.

Cafe Royale

Index

Index